EntreBalance

EntreBalance

Principles to Balance Your Life and Pursue an Entrepreneurial Mindset

Jared Polak

LUCIDBOOKS

Houston, Texas

EntreBalance: Principles to Balance Your Life and Pursue an
Entrepreneurial Mindset

Published by Lucid Books in Brenham, TX.
www.LucidBooks.net

First Printing 2013

ISBN-13: 978-1-935909-71-2
ISBN-10: 1935909711

Special Sales: Most Lucid Books titles are available in special quantity
discounts. Custom imprinting or excerpting can also be done to fit
special needs. Contact Lucid Books at info@lucidbooks.net.

TABLE OF CONTENTS

PREFACE TO BOOK

One could argue that one of the most important necessities in life is water. Water covers over 70% of the Earth, and the human body is made up of nearly 60% water. It surrounds us, fuels us, and keeps us alive. But it's not just any type of water that's important to our existence and survival. It's *clean* water. *Fresh* water. *Pure* water.

Perhaps this is why so many metaphors found in literature, philosophy, and religion revolve around water. It flows through our consciousness in the same way a river cuts a line through the land. In this way, water fuels our stories and our thoughts just like it fuels our lives. Metaphorically, our search for contentment in life can be seen as a search for clean water.

In January of 2006, I decided to leave a management position at a large company to travel the world and help the poor. According to conventional wisdom, it was an illogical decision. Although many people thought it was noble to want to serve others, they couldn't understand why I would walk away from upward mobility and job security.

The benefits were immediate, however. My life quickly changed from overworked, overwhelmed, and unbalanced to excessive amounts of free time and the ability to live out my life passions. It was spectacular.

It was also short-lived.

I had noble ideas but lacked effective planning. I soon ran out of the resources necessary to take care of my own basic needs. I came to the hard realization that I couldn't effectively serve other people if I was unable to buy food, shelter, and clothing for myself. It didn't take me long to figure out that money is just as important as time and can be used as a valuable tool to serve more people.

From that low point came a new focus on creating enough time and money in my own life to be able to provide for family and myself, live a balanced life, and serve people. I had a passion and urgency to join a company or start a business that would help others achieve their own unique dreams. I was driven by the desire to wake up every morning in love with my life and work. I decided to start a coaching company that helps people earn more money professionally while maintaining balance in their lives. I originally began working with owners, managers, multi-level marketers, or self-employed professionals in the small business community. I began to help this group by providing a process that improved their businesses, while giving them a model that could help them achieve their life dreams.

I ran into another problem. My business grew to

full capacity. There was a limited amount of coaching hours per day and an unlimited amount of people that I wanted to serve. That's when I decided to change the way I shared my coaching with the world. My dream was to create high value content that I could share in a variety of different ways. This book is one such way.

Although the following story is fiction, it is centered on timeless truths along with new concepts that go against commonly held beliefs. I have provided the following website: www.JaredPolak.com for additional support. It will help you strategically apply the big ideas of this book to bring successful change to your life.

Please join me for this adventure. I hope that what you find in these pages is as refreshing as a glass of clean water.

Warmest Regards,

Jared Polak

CHAPTER 1

Mark Davis settled into his chair in the waiting room as if he already owned the place. The doors to the executive office were closed, but Mark knew who would be on the other side: Jim Brenner, Scott Jesse, Stuart Francis, and John Henry. They were the president and vice presidents of Johnston Beverage Distributors, the company Mark worked for. Although many had sat in the chair before him, waiting anxiously to discover their fate with the company, Mark had no reason to be nervous. He was confident that the meeting he was about to attend was the first step in his promotion to vice president.

The president's administrative assistant smiled an apology to Mark. "I'm sorry Mr. Brenner's a little late in meeting with you. I think he's on a conference call with Mr. Johnston."

Mark grinned. "No need to apologize, I'm in no rush, Kim." Mr. Johnston himself was involved, further proof that good news was on the other side of the door.

"By the way, congratulations on your award, Mr. Davis. It's a good looking watch."

Mark allowed himself another glance at his reward for being named "Employee of the Decade." "Good looking" did not come close to describing its sleek beauty. The watch was an 18 carat gold Perrelet Turbine XL, complete with a ceramic bezel and clear backing. The papers included with the watch informed Mark of two key features. The first was that it was a limited edition piece; only 77 existed in the world. The second was that it was worth at least $20,000. Although both features were notable, what impressed Mark most was the fact that he knew of only four other people who wore Perrelet watches: the men he was about to meet with.

As Kim answered a phone call, Mark took in his surroundings. The walls of the waiting room were dominated by two massive bookshelves full of motivational titles. He started to count the number of books with the word "success" printed on the spine, but gave up after entering the double digits. One title caught his attention: *Backpacking Through El Salvador.* It was completely out of place on the shelf and looked as if it had never been touched. He had the fleeting thought that maybe the book had been placed there specifically for him to notice, that there was some hidden message that only he could decipher. Mark shook the thought out of his head.

Mark had read many of the motivational books in his years with the company, but he already knew the true equation that had led him to that waiting room: success = sacrifice.

The sacrifices had started out small. When Mark

began his career as a merchandiser for local grocery accounts, it had been the long hours and verbal abuse typical of being at the bottom of the corporate ladder. In his acceptance speech for his award the week before, he had recounted some of those battles. There had been the grocery store employee who had forced Mark to do his own job for a week, cleaning the bathrooms and sorting shipments, until Mark stood up and put him in his place. There were the endless hours driving in the car when he listened to audiobooks on sales and memorized every closing technique mentioned. There were the holidays he missed due to impending sales and friendships that were replaced by long hours.

Robert McNally, his best friend since elementary school, had finally stopped calling to set up hang out times. The last time Mark heard from him was in an e-mail from over a year ago. It was more of a rant than a message—listing all the ways Mark had let him down over the years. Although Mark was sad to lose his friend, it was a relief to know that he would no longer have to deal with the tinge of guilt that came with every voicemail Robert left.

But it was in the midst of those sacrifices that Mark crafted his vision for moving up in the company, and it was his drive to win "Employee of the Decade" and secure a spot as future vice president that kept him afloat.

The bigger and more recent sacrifices mostly involved his wife and two kids. It was uncomfortable for Mark to think about, so he occupied his mind with possible responses to the announcement of his new position.

The doors to the executive office creaked open to reveal Mr. Brenner. He was dressed immaculately in a Gucci 2-button suit that made Mark's Calvin Kline 3-piece seem casual in comparison.

"Sorry to keep you waiting, Mark. Mr. Johnston called in last minute. He sends his congratulations for your award."

"That means a lot to me, Mr. Brenner. Thank you for taking the time to meet with me."

"Come in."

Mr. Brenner held the door for Mark as he entered the office. The vice presidents were already seated at their posts around the heavy mahogany table that was the centerpiece of the room. Mark had seen the room in passing many times during the course of his career, but this was the first time he had been invited inside.

"Please, take a seat."

Mr. Brenner gestured towards the chair next to him. Mark sat and almost had to check to make sure he was actually seated. The leather executive chair he sank into formed perfectly to the shape of his body, making it feel like he was suspended in the air. He hid his awe at the luxury of the room and focused on his posture. It was important the men knew he was not intimidated.

"Mark," Mr. Brenner began, "you have been an invaluable asset to the company, which is why you were chosen as the Employee of the Decade. Your loyalty and dedication to excellence have been consistent throughout your tenure. As you are well aware, Scott, Stuart, and John have all been winners of the award, and I'm sure you have been anticipating the day when you too will become a vice president."

"Yes, sir. That's been a personal goal of mine since I started with the company."

"And I'm sure you're aware of John's upcoming retirement as vice president."

"Yes, sir. Congratulations, Mr. Henry."

"Thank you, Mark."

Mark noticed that Mr. Henry did not look at him as he spoke, and he figured that the retirement was an awkward subject. He made a mental note to be careful not to mention it to him again.

Mr. Brenner continued. "I've had numerous conversations with Mr. Johnston about who is to replace John as vice president. They have been difficult conversations, which is why we were late in meeting with you today."

Mark couldn't contain his smile any longer, but he realized it seemed to make the men uncomfortable.

"Mark, I prefer to be frank about this. Mr. Johnston has expressed his desire to replace John with his grandson, Daniel."

The smile remained plastered on Mark's face as his mind raced to process the news. "His grandson?"

"As you're aware, Daniel has only been with the company for five years, and we didn't expect him to be ready for a vice president position for another ten. Although he is not qualified on paper, this is Mr. Johnston's vision for his grandson and the company."

His smile disappeared as Mark clenched his jaw. He spoke softly and slowly to keep his mounting anger from showing. "So I'll have to wait to receive my promotion?"

"Well, that's the other news we wanted to meet

with you about. According to Mr. Johnston, Scott and Stuart will most likely eventually be replaced by his other grandson and granddaughter."

Mark's stomach reeled as he tried to look for the hole in the conversation—the gap in logic he could plug and save everything from rushing down the drain. "So you'll create a new vice presidential position for me? I can help guide them since they'll need to learn the ropes."

Mr. Henry leaned back in his chair and spoke. "Mark, that can't happen. The company doesn't have the revenue for another position."

"Can't you do something?"

"As I said, this is Mr. Johnston's vision for the company," Mr. Brenner said. "We are sorry to have to tell you this. Believe me, we're as frustrated as you."

With his palms firmly pressed against the smooth finish of the table, Mark tried to order the whirlpool of thoughts, emotions, and protests swirling through his mind. "You have no idea how frustrated I am. What about future opportunities for promotion?"

Mr. Brenner cleared his throat. "You know that we value you tremendously, Mark. You deserve the award you won many times over. We would like you to maintain a high-level of performance with your current position."

Mark choked out a laugh. "My current position? That's it?"

"I believe you have some vacation saved up. Take some days off and think through all of this. Remember that you have an excellent position here. A position many people would covet."

Is that a threat, Mark thought. He felt like he had

just been blindsided by a punch to the head. "Do you have any other surprises for me?"

"No," said the President, "that will be all."

Mark exited the room briskly, not bothering to shut the door. The administrative assistant smiled and began to say something, but he cut her off by yanking his coat from its hook. He concentrated all the anger, pain, and confusion he was feeling into one look at Kim, and she withered away from his gaze, pretending to write on her calendar.

Mark made it out of the building in record time. He couldn't help slamming the door to the parking garage as he exited the building. His confidence and excitement leaked out of him with every step, and a mixture of horror and confusion filled the vacancies. He was an untethered boat, drifting out into the storm. The promotion to vice president had been his focus for so many years that he didn't know what to do next.

His life was over.

Mark climbed into his car and rested his head against the steering wheel to fight the waves of nausea that threatened to overtake him. After twenty years in the company, he had reached his ceiling in the business: an expensive watch and a pat on the back.

CHAPTER 2

Mark drove around his block three times before pulling into his driveway. With his fingers on the door handle, he thought of how he would explain the meeting to Veronica, which was enough to make him put the car in reverse for a couple more loops around the neighborhood. It's not that he had a hard time communicating with his wife; he was used to bragging to his maritally dysfunctional friends about the straightforward and honest system they had of speaking with one another. The problem was one of expectations. Mark had been promising Veronica the impending promotion for years. Every time he missed a school event for his son or daughter in order to close a sale, he reminded Veronica of why he was working so hard. His explanation for why he couldn't commit to a weekly date night was summed up in two words: vice president. She had even taken to calling him VP every once in awhile, although it was usually laced with a sharp-edged sarcasm.

As a salesman, Mark knew the importance of following through on what you have promised. And he knew not to make promises unless it was a sure thing. He had the watch on his wrist and the meeting with his bosses; it had looked liked a sure thing.

Veronica was going to kill him.

On his sixth trip around the block, Mark thought of his out. He almost started laughing at the brilliance of his plan. It was sure to buy him at least the evening, which would allow him enough time to think of a new spin to his situation. The only challenge would be not letting any of the anger that was rippling through his body show.

Mark parked the car and walked up to his doorway, taking deep breaths while imagining Mr. Johnston in a cage-fight with a professional kick boxer. The door opened before he had a chance to touch its handle.

"Did it happen? Are you a VP?" Veronica stood before him, gushing excitement.

"There will be plenty of time for all of that later. We've got somewhere to be."

"What are you talking about?"

"Wasn't there that missionary thing at church you wanted to go to?"

Mark almost felt guilty as Veronica jumped through the doorway and embraced him. "You mean you'll come to church with us tonight?"

"Of course."

"Well, if this is the kind of free time a new VP has, it's worth the years of waiting.

"I always knew it would be." Mark decided the cage-fight was too merciful for Mr. Johnston. He adjusted his mind's eye so that Mr. Johnston was now swimming with some sharks.

And there was blood in the water.

⚖

As he walked with his family through the main entrance to Good News Methodist Church, Mark noticed details that had slipped by unseen in the ten years they had been members. There was a crack in the wood of the main door that leaked out yellow light from the inner sanctuary. A bench in the back of the room was sectioned off with the purple velvet ropes found in old movie theaters. Even the quiet acoustic guitar strums of the worship pastor sounded heavier, resonating deep inside Mark's head. He wondered if this was how prisoners felt on death row; everything around them taking on a new vibrancy and significance. He snuck a quick glance at Veronica, and she was beaming.

Mark had mixed feelings about using church to mislead his wife. He was pretty sure there were similar stories in the Bible that ended with fatal lightning strikes or horrible famines. After taking a tentative step or two down the aisle, Mark realized he wasn't going to be struck dead, at least not immediately, and he began to breathe a little easier.

The family settled into their usual spot near the front. There was a table set up near the pastor's lectern, which Mark figured was for communion. Pastor Randy stood and went through his usual greeting: joke, serious note, welcome. Mark relaxed into the familiar routine as if it were a well-worn easy chair. Church had always been a place where he could peacefully turn off his mind, and he found it hard to continue his violent fantasies against Mr. Johnston and his grandchildren in God's house.

Pastor Randy finished his greeting and introduced the night's special speaker. It was an old man with a white beard that Mark didn't recognize. He was dressed in cargo pants and a white polo shirt that had some type of agricultural equipment embroidered over the pocket. He looked out of place in the formality of the sanctuary.

"Good evening, church," the man began. "Tonight I'm going to talk to you about something we all take for granted. It's something that we have in abundance but that the majority of the world lacks."

Money, thought Mark.

"Clean water," the man continued. He held up Pastor Randy's familiar cup full of water that rested on the lectern. "This cup of water is the difference between life and death for many children around the world."

The man poured the water out onto the stage. There was a gasp from somewhere in the congregation. "But we waste this God-given resource without batting an eyelash."

"Now, I don't have time to get into the clean-water crisis in the *entire* world, so my goal tonight is to open your eyes to the situation in one particular country, a country I know and love. El Salvador."

The name of the country rippled through Mark. He remembered the book in the waiting room and again felt as if there was a hidden message just for him. He was uneasy with how the name lodged itself in his brain like an annoying sliver of wood. There was no way for him to leave without drawing Veronica's attention and suspicion, so Mark resigned to do what he always did in church: he closed his eyes and tried to sleep.

A light tapping on his knee turned into a hard pinch, and Mark awoke with a start. Veronica was angrily motioning for him to exit the row, and he realized that everyone was filing towards the front of the sanctuary. Communion time.

He smiled sheepishly at Veronica, but she was already gathering up the kids. Mark stood and stretched, feeling refreshed. He knew he would have to tell Veronica the bad news tomorrow, but he felt optimistic. He could always find a new job, one where the ceiling wasn't so low. Or he could call up his lawyer and find out if he could sue the company for nepotism. He was fairly certain there was an anti-nepotism policy in his contract, which could give him grounds for charging them with breach of contract. As he shuffled towards the front of the church with the rest of the congregation, Mark allowed himself a tentative smile.

Lost in his plans for the future, he didn't realize that there wasn't any bread being offered at the communion table. He picked up the glass from the tabletop, barely noticing that it wasn't the usual brass cup. The liquid had a strange, earthy scent as he brought it to his lips and took a giant gulp.

"Mark, what are you doing?" Veronica's voice was

tinged with panic, and for a second Mark thought he had spilled some of the wine on his Burberry dress shirt.

The taste of the wine finally registered, and it wasn't a flavor he recognized. He had to swallow again to keep from retching. He looked down at the glass he was still holding and realized that it held a brown liquid that was definitely not wine.

"This isn't communion?"

Veronica took the glass out of his hand, and he noticed her hands were shaking. "That was part of the demonstration. He brought the water to give us a visual. You just drank the dirty water from El Salvador."

El Salvador. The word heaved from Mark's ears to his toes and back again. Images of dead animals floating in the water played out in front of his face. His knees wobbled and he saw spots floating in his vision.

"Help, is anyone a doctor?" Veronica's voice sounded far away and tinny.

Mark's stomach pitched as he doubled over. *Maybe this is my punishment,* he thought. *Lightning would be less embarrassing.*

Then he passed out.

CHAPTER 3

Something was snaking through Mark's nostrils and down his throat. He tried to scream but the darkness surrounding his head filled his mouth before he could utter a sound. His flailing arms found something solid, and he pushed up, trying to get away.

A rush of warm air finally reached his lungs and Mark exploded with a series of retching coughs. Rolling over onto his back, he opened his eyes to find himself staring at an expansive, cloudless sky. It was daytime. A puddle was directly to his left, and he realized that he must have been face down and drowning in it just moments before. Blinking the muddy water from his eyes, he sat up shakily to take in his surroundings.

Good News Methodist Church was nowhere to be seen.

Mark slicked his hair back and tried to remember where he was. There was the old guy with the beard and the funny-tasting communion wine. He remembered

Veronica's hands shaking. Then it hit him. *He drank the water!*

The thought triggered a new series of dry heaves that ended with Mark clutching his stomach in pain. Where *was* he?

The puddle sat in the middle of a vast field of dirt. The ground was light brown and a bit dusty; Mark realized with a groan that he was covered in it. He could see a tree line in the distance to his left, and with more dirt stretching out to the right, he figured the trees were as good a destination as any.

With each step towards the trees, Mark tried to piece together what he was doing in the field. His surroundings didn't look like any place he had been to in Texas, and he had travelled all over the state. The dirt and trees reminded him more of Mexico. Mark didn't understand how he had gone from accidentally drinking bad water in church to waking up in a puddle. As far as he could tell, he was alone.

After wracking his brain for the entire twenty minute walk to the tree line, Mark had convinced himself that danger was all around him. He plopped down on a clump of grass and tried to slow his breathing.

Crack. It was not the type of sound Mark wanted to hear. Snap. He frantically searched the ground in front of him for a pointed stick or rock—anything that could possibly injure a man or wild beast. There was a pile of mud by his feet and Mark scooped a handful, ready to throw it in the eyes of anything that crossed his path.

Suddenly, a man appeared from behind a nearby

tree trunk. Mark was too startled to throw his mud. The man didn't look dangerous. He had a tan, leathery face and silver hair. His well-worn jeans and flannel shirt draped comfortably over his lanky body, and he was sipping from one of those water packs you wear on your back.

The man gestured to Mark's raised hand while still sipping from the nozzle attached to his backpack. He reattached the nozzle to the shoulder of his pack and said, "Hey brother, what's that all about?"

Mark's mind suddenly went blank. It was as if he had so many questions that his brain had to reboot. "It's mud. I was going to throw it in your eyes."

The man laughed. "That's not mud, my friend."

The realization was a long time coming. Then Mark burst into action, shaking the "mud" from his palm and streaking his hand against the grass.

The tall man leaned against a tree trunk and watched. "I guess this is your first time in El Salvador."

Mark froze. "What did you say?"

"I was just saying you look like this is your first time in El Salvador."

"El Salvador?" Mark managed to choke the words out of his constricted chest. His feet seemed to come loose from the ground. He was a balloon caught in a sudden updraft.

"Whoa, you're not looking too good right now." The man pushed off of the tree trunk and caught Mark as he stumbled forward. "You should drink some of my water."

It was the word *water*, with all its recent history, that popped the balloon version of Mark. Although he had a million questions that needed immediate answers, Mark could only do what he had grown pretty good at recently.

He passed out.

⚖

M ark awoke for the second time that day dizzy and disoriented. His blurred vision slowly focused on the old man's face gazing inquisitively into his own. It wasn't until he tried to sit up that Mark realized he was sitting in a bed.

"Don't worry, I washed your hands for you already," the man said. His voice was low and rough, like thunder in the distance. "You've been out for awhile."

"Where am I?" Mark asked. It took all the dwindling strength he had to not mentally shut out the answer.

"You're at our base camp in San Sebastián Salitrillo, friend. El Salvador."

"Not possible. I'm supposed to be in Texas."

A smile cracked across the old man's face, another crease in the leather. "Are you sure? The team said they were one man short, we prayed, and here you are."

"The team?"

"The drill team. I think one or two of them are from Texas."

Mark tried to stand and instantly started listing to one side. The old man grabbed him and leaned him against the wall. His grip was surprisingly firm.

"Thanks…"

"Juan."

"Thank you Juan. I'm Mark." Mark pushed himself

off the wall and regained his balance. "Now, where's your phone."

B ase camp turned out to be more camp than base. The room Mark walked out of was a tiny offshoot of a small dining area enclosed within four short concrete walls. Outside the bunker were a number of tents, a haphazard littering of hunter-green domes. Finding a phone proved difficult.

There were no phone lines leading out to the camp, and although each of the team members had cell phones (and were all Americans, to Mark's relief), no one was receiving any type of service. The quest to find a phone was a good excuse for Mark to meet the rest of the team. He was surprised to find himself curious about all the Americans in the middle of nowhere in El Salvador. Why would anyone *willingly* come to be a part of a "drill team," whatever that was? He was even more surprised when the team looked like a collection of confident, put-together business people rather than the longhaired Peace Corps dropouts he was expecting.

There was Jeremy, an athletic man in his mid-30's who had the easy grin and firm handshake of someone who was experienced in sales. Theresa was a bubbly, talkative woman in her late-20's who had the free spirit Mark usually associated with entrepreneurs. Sandra spoke to Mark with precise diction and had a regal beauty about her that screamed money, Ivy League, and maybe a house in the Hamptons. Thomas, who everyone called Uncle Thomas for some reason, was a vivacious old man with white hair who seemed to be in the running with Juan in the "old man with huge personality" contest. Finally, there was Tanner. His hair was long and he was wearing a dusty leather jacket that was only missing the back patch of a biker gang, but he offered Mark the warmest greeting and even joined in his search for a working cell phone.

"I see you've met our motley crew," Juan said, approaching Mark in the midst of the tents.

"Yeah, they're great. I just wish one of them had a working cell phone."

Juan grinned, flashing a set of immaculate teeth. "Well, like I said, we have been waiting for one more team member."

"I'm sure they'll show up. I have to get back to Texas."

"Why?"

The question startled Mark. How could this man *not* understand that he shouldn't be in El Salvador?

"Not that it's any of your business, but I have a lot to take care of in Texas. I just found out that I won't be receiving a well-deserved promotion due to nepotism, so there's a meeting with my lawyer. I also have about 15 accounts that I'm in charge of that have a major sale approaching. If those accounts are left in the hands of anyone else in the company, they're sure to be lost sales since I'm the only one competent enough to handle them. Oh, and did I also mention that I have absolutely *no idea* how I ended up in the middle of nowhere El Salvador in the first place?"

Mark could feel the panic settling in, and he took a deep breath. Juan walked up to him and put a hand on his shoulder. Mark's impulse was to flinch away,

Chapter 3

but the hand was unexpectedly reassuring. It was as if Juan were rooting him to the ground. It was the first time Mark had felt even a pinch of peace since finding himself in the unfamiliar country.

"Do you have any family back in Texas?" Juan asked.

"A wife and two children."

"Hmmm."

A thick knot of guilt settled in the back of Mark's stomach. He hadn't even mentioned them. All of his reasons for wanting to get back to Texas were work related...*Mark* related. It was as if he had peeked behind the curtain to see what was really going on backstage. And what he found was a man who was more worried about a job that had already betrayed him than his own family.

"It sounds like you have many things to think about," Juan said after a moment.

"I guess I do."

"And you have many responsibilities back home."

"That's putting it mildly."

"So what are you working so hard for?"

There were many answers Mark wanted to give. *Family. Purpose. Teamwork.* But he had the funny feeling Juan would see right through him. "Money," he answered sheepishly.

"Of course. Not many people are so ready to admit it, but money is the driving factor in all our work. But have you ever thought about *why* you want all the money?"

Images of a new car, long, white beaches, and gourmet meals flashed through Mark's mind. "To enjoy it," he said.

"Can you remember when you last had the *time* to enjoy your money?"

Mark thought. Then he thought hard. All he could conjure were memories of long weekends working accounts and Sundays spent with his laptop open on the table.

"I guess it's been awhile," he finally answered.

Juan began walking through the middle of the tents. He paused and waited for Mark to follow. "I believe that I can help you, Mark, if you're interested."

Mark gave what he hoped was a non-committal shrug.

"As you can see from my hair and wrinkles, I've got some years in me. And those years have taught me many things. One thing I learned long ago was that **money, without time, is useless**."

Mark bit the inside of his cheeks to try to suppress his grin, but was unsuccessful. *Great, a Salvadoran guru*, he thought to himself. They stopped beside one of the tents.

"It's okay if you're skeptical. Everyone here was skeptical at first." Juan slapped the side of the tent with his palm. "Jeremy, can you come out for a moment?"

The front flap of the tent zipped open, and Jeremy stretched his body out. He swept his blonde hair to the side and shook Mark's hand once more.

"Jeremy's in sales, too," Juan said.

"I had already guessed," Mark said.

Jeremy laughed. "Takes one to know one."

"Jeremy used to pour himself into his job, just like you," Juan continued. "He's sells luxury cars, and he even used to sleep in them overnight so that he could truthfully and accurately speak to the comfortable interiors."

"I slept like a baby every time," Jeremy added.

"The dedication paid off. Jeremy started averaging $28,000 a month and was able to afford an apartment with a view of the Dallas skyline, like the ones you see in movies. He was working close to 80 hours a week and making more money than he knew what to do with. I'll let him tell the rest."

"Sounds like you were living the dream life," Mark said.

"That's what I thought too," Jeremy replied. "I was making a ton of money, but the long hours were wearing me down. I wasn't happy with the schedule. I felt compelled to keep working because of my school and credit card debts. My father kept calling to check in on me, and he warned me that I needed to slow down. I hadn't been home to see my family for well over a year. Then my dad had a stroke. I couldn't take time off for another month, and when I went to see him, it was like he was a shell of the man he used to be. I hated myself for not seeing him sooner, and I hated my job for stealing all of my time. I realized that in my quest to make my money, I had alienated myself from everyone who mattered in my life. I decided to reprioritize my life right there at my parents' house. I had one day to plan, which was enough. I created a list of low value items in my life and I eliminated them to free up more time. I started by giving away my TV."

"Just like that?" Mark asked.

"It was hard at first, but I came to love the extra time I had to spend with friends and family. "

"Let me guess," Mark interrupted. "Next you cut down on your hours so you could have more time to do whatever you wanted to do."

"Good guess. Wrong, but good. I worked even *harder* than before. I knew that by working hard and long hours up front, I could free up more time later. I also figured that part of the reason I felt so compelled to work non-stop was due to the burden of my debts. I paid off $110,000 of school debt in six months."

"Whoa."

"With less financial stress, I could finally choose to work less with a clean conscience. And I found that I began to enjoy my job *more*. The quality of my work increased, and I ended up making the same amount of sales in much less time. I was also able to start helping out here in El Salvador multiple times a year."

"You've probably already heard Juan's 'money, without time, is useless' spiel," Jeremy continued. "At one point, in my youthful ignorance, I would have scoffed. But it's true. I had to learn it the hard way."

"How is drilling for oil helping out?" Mark asked.

Juan and Jeremy looked at each other with raised eyebrows. Then they both erupted with laughter. Soon they were doubled over and slapping each other's backs. Mark was worried they were about to start rolling on the ground.

"What's so funny?"

"We're not drilling for oil," Jeremy said, wiping a tear from his eye. "We're drilling wells for clean water. We're trying to help the villages."

Warmth spread through Mark's cheeks. "That was my next guess," he said.

"This is why we need you, Mark," Jeremy said. "It's an involved process, and every team member is essential. We can't do it if we're missing someone."

"This will give you time to think," Juan added. "I've always found manual labor to be a good time to think."

Mark didn't want to admit it to himself, but he *was* curious. He had never really participated in anything so humanitarian, and it *would* look good on his résumé if he ended up quitting his job at Johnston. Besides, everyone seemed nice, even Juan with his self-styled guru-ing. "I'll think about it," he said.

Juan and Jeremy gave each other a high-five as if it was already settled. "We managed to get a computer hooked up through a satellite if you wanted to try to write home," Juan said. "It's pretty primitive, but at least you can send a message out or purchase a ticket home."

"And the tent next door is all yours," Jeremy added. "I left you some more appropriate work clothing inside."

"Thank you. Both of you. I really appreciate it." Mark was used to expressing gratitude. It was a part of his job. This time was different, though. This time he sincerely meant it.

⚖️

The soft glow of the laptop screen lit up Mark's face. His fingers were on the keyboard and he had a message box open, but he didn't know what to write.

He thought about everything Jeremy had shared with him. It was true—Mark was making a lot of money. But he didn't have any time. He always felt so busy and rushed.

The memory drifted through his mind like a cloud.

He was at Disney World with his family three years ago. He had managed to squeeze in a three-day weekend and was able to catch a glimpse of what more time with his family could be like. They were walking through the crowds, making their way to Space Mountain. One hand was gently holding the hand of his daughter; the other was holding Veronica's, fingers entwined. Their son ran ahead, shouting out everything he saw with excitement and delight. Veronica kissed him on the cheek, and Mark couldn't believe how lucky he was to be able to spend time with such an amazing family. He loved them.

Before the memory could twist away, Mark pounded out a quick e-mail to Veronica.

Veronica,

I have no idea how it happened, but I am in El Salvador. Please do not worry about me. I met a team of Americans who are drilling clean water wells for the villagers. I have some vacation days saved up, and I want to stay and help. Please call work and let them know I am taking a few days off.

With Love,

Mark

⚖

M ark found a change of clothes waiting for him on his sleeping bag in the tent. He also saw an old leather journal with a pen. He cracked it open to find it full of blank pages. He hadn't written anything other than work reports and e-mails in many years, but he had the sudden urge to document his day. After all, he had somehow ended up on a well drilling team in El Salvador—there had to be some reason for it.

He opened the journal to the first page and wrote:

> ### EntreBalance Principle #1:
> **Money is useless without time.**

EntreBalance Principles

1. Money is useless without time.

CHAPTER 4

There wasn't any rooster crowing to wake Mark up in the morning. Instead, it sounded like every other animal in existence *besides* a rooster was prancing around outside of his tent. Mark spent half the night trying to identify the squealing, guttural sounds he was hearing; the only one that was easily identifiable was Jeremy's snoring from the tent next door. He found himself wishing there was a soundproof luxury car for Jeremy to sleep in. At some point he must have drifted off, because he awoke with a start, convinced some jaguar/mountain lion crossbreed was slicing through the side of his tent with a massive claw.

ZZZzzzzziiiiippppp.

Mark jammed himself into the far corner of his tent and pulled his sleeping bag over his head.

"Good morning, Mark. Are you awake? I have coffee." Juan's too-cheerful voice sounded from the front of his tent.

"Did you say coffee?" Mark slowly peeled the

sleeping bag from his head and grinned sheepishly at Juan. "I thought you were a jaguar."

"You don't have to worry about jaguars here, my friend," Juan said, reassuringly. "Our problem is snakes."

Mark pulled on his borrowed work clothes, shaking each piece of clothing to make sure no sleeping snakes were hidden in the folds. He followed Juan to the mess bunker, stepping gingerly and watching his feet the entire way.

⚖

B reakfast consisted of eggs and toast. Mark was surprised and disappointed to discover that the promised coffee was instant. He tried to hide his disdain as he choked down the acidic dregs.

"It's awful, isn't it?" said Theresa, who was sitting beside him.

"Horrible. Atrocious. Tragic."

"I know. I would have thought Central America would be chock full of great coffee since they're the ones importing all of it to us. I mean, I pay like fifteen bucks a pound for coffee from El Salvador back home. And then here, all they drink is Nescafe."

"I haven't had this stuff since I was in college. It tastes like a hangover."

Theresa choked out a laugh and splashed some of her coffee over the table. "That's great, I'm stealing that."

"So, do you know what my job's going to be with the drilling?" Mark asked.

"I don't know. Has Juan done his thing with you yet?"

"His thing? Um…"

"You're going to need to take a little trip with him first. Then we'll talk shop."

"What kind of trip?" Mark tried to wash down his nervousness with another swig of the coffee.

"You'll have to wait and see for yourself," Theresa answered, raising her eyebrows. "I don't want to ruin the surprise."

"It's okay, I'm kind of sick of surprises."

"Be sick of stuff like this coffee, Mark. Don't ever get sick of *surprises*. They're life's way of showing us new ways to look at things."

She had a point, but Mark wasn't sure he was ready for any more new ways to look at things. Wasn't magically appearing in a puddle in the middle of El Salvador enough?

"Mark!" Juan called from the other end of the room. "I hope you have your hiking boots on. We're going on a journey."

The unsettled feeling was back in the bottom of Mark's stomach, swimming in the pool of instant coffee. Everyone in the room was looking at him with knowing expressions.

"Here's your chance for a new way to look at things," Theresa said.

"Yeah, great," Mark mumbled as he joined Juan at the door to the bunker. *I better not have to sniff tree bark or kill a deer with my bare hands*, he thought.

"This isn't some ancient ritual," Juan said, reading his mind. "We're just going to a place of questions."

"I hate to break it to you, but this whole place has been nothing but questions." Mark was proud of his retort; unfortunately, it fell on nothing but air. Juan was already blazing a trail through the forest.

⚖

It turned out that there already was a trail; it was just easy to miss. The trail was a thin trickle of dirt that flowed through the dense foliage of the forest. The dirt was packed tough and the split ends of branches and vines framed their heads as they walked. Every couple of minutes, Juan would pause to hack at encroaching foliage with a rusty machete. Mark tried not to think about all the hacking and slashing, but recurring images of being a human sacrifice in the middle of the forest poked into his mind with every *whoosh* of the blade.

That was why he was gratefully relieved when Juan started using their hike as a time to share his own life story. Juan relayed how he had grown up in El Salvador in a wealthy family. He had studied mechanical engineering at MIT and had immediately found prosperity and success in the oil and gas business. His knowledge of Central American culture combined with his US education and business savvy to make him one of the most sought-after engineers in his field. His twenties were a blur of excess and affluence, but the luster of life started to dull as he entered his thirties.

"The problem was a problem of philosophy," Juan explained. "I had a great life—anything I ever wanted. But I began to feel restless. It just didn't seem to mean anything."

"But you were successful," Mark said. "What about your prestige?"

"Don't get me wrong, it was great to a point. But I had all these questions that plagued me at night. Why am I here? What's the point to life? Is there anything after death? Everyone in my social circles had some type of answer, usually something they had read in college. But I could tell they all worried about it at night as well. It was like we were all going around wearing our success like a mask—underneath we were all just scared or drifting."

Although he didn't want to, Mark couldn't help but think of his own life. He thought of the business lunches, the late nights wining and dining potential clients. There was always a tinge of desperation, as if they were trying to ward off something dark and sinister—death or old age.

"I remembered some of the lower-class people who I grew up around," Juan continued. "I was always annoyed by how 'God' was their answer to everything. But as I sat up at night, haunted by those questions, it really struck me how those poor people seemed to have a peace that I lacked, even though their lives were much harder than my own."

"Yeah, but didn't that peace seem a little naïve? I mean, it could've been just a lack of education or a simplistic outlook on life."

"That's what I told myself on those late nights. But I was never fully satisfied. It always felt like empty rationalization."

"So what'd you do?"

"I finally caved in and sought out an old friend from my days at MIT. His name was Jack, and we were roommates enrolled in the same program. He always annoyed me because he was better at everything. Except, halfway through the program, he dropped out and enrolled in seminary. I was furious and felt that it was a complete waste of his talent, but he insisted that it was God's direction for his life."

"I hate when people say things like that."

"I did too, my friend. It seemed so abstract and impractical. Yet, it was Jack who I sought out in that dark time of my life. We started reading through the Bible together, and he showed me the answers to those heavy questions. The answers didn't always make sense in my head, but they made sense in my heart."

"So…you found God?"

Juan laughed. "You don't have to sound so nervous. I am not here to evangelize you, Mark. I am just helping you understand the path that led me back to El Salvador. Just like this thin little line through the forest, my path has had many unexpected turns."

"Was that it? Did all of those questions go away in some magical *poof*?" Mark asked.

"Far from it. I still wasn't done asking questions. Although I felt a newfound peace, I couldn't help but ask myself, 'What next? Now that I believe in the God of the Bible, what does that mean for me here on earth? What's my purpose?'"

Juan paused to hack at some more foliage while Mark chewed on his story. He didn't want to admit it, but Juan's story was resonating something deep inside of his heart. As they continued down the path, he confessed, "I ask myself the same thing all the time. What answer did you find?"

Juan grinned. "That would be too easy. Besides,

my answer probably won't help much. Everyone has to find their own answers."

"So there's no shortcut?"

"If there was, I would be a millionaire from selling it." Juan stopped on the trail and turned his full attention back to Mark, looking at him with a new type of intensity. "There's a reason you're here in El Salvador, Mark. Maybe you'll find some answers. The place I want to show you has helped many of my friends answer questions about purpose and meaning."

"Wait, this sounds like a shortcut."

Juan let out a single laugh that sounded like a handclap. "I would call it more of a place to reflect."

"So I don't owe you a million dollars?"

"This one's for free."

⚖

The rest of their journey down the path was blanketed by silence. The only sounds were the crackling brush or occasional birdcall. Mark began to ask himself some difficult questions regarding his wife, his children, and the overall direction of his life. He pictured his life as a straight line, boxed in on either side by career and success. But he wasn't sure where the line was leading him. He used to think it was wealth and recognition at the end of the line, but now he wasn't so sure.

After walking about two more miles, the men approached a small church with a playground on the right for children, a concrete basketball court behind it, and a cemetery on the left. Upon approaching the church, Mark had the sinking feeling that they would be entering the cemetery.

"I'm guessing we're not here to listen to a sermon or play basketball," Mark said.

"You're nervous about the cemetery, my friend?" Juan had reached the border and was beckoning Mark forward. "Don't worry, Mark. El Salvador's ghosts are not the type to hang out in old cemeteries."

"It just seems a bit…rude. I don't know any of these people."

"Every life is like a signpost to us as we seek meaning. Some lives inspire us to greatness, others lead us to pain and despair. It's the same with death. It's often only after death that the true value of a life can be determined."

Mark hesitated at the grassy border of the cemetery. "That's great philosophy and all, Juan. But we're still about to walk over a bunch of dead people."

"Well, if you don't want to view it philosophically, we can try a different way of looking at it: Quit hesitating and be a man!" Juan grabbed Mark's arm and pulled him into the cemetery. "I promise this place can provide some answers."

Mark stumbled into the cemetery, pulled along by Juan. His shock gave way to laughter, and soon both men were chuckling. The tension was gone. But as they walked farther into the cemetery, winding between the tombstones, the mood turned somber. They settled into silence once more. The only sound was the dry grass crackling beneath their feet.

"I want you to wander around a bit," Juan said. "Try to answer this question: What are some of the characteristics of these tombstones? Regardless of the size, shape, or color of the tombstone, what's similar throughout?"

Mark stared at several different tombstones and walked around the small grassy yard several times. He started to really think about the question. As Mark walked around, he thought about his mother, who died of breast cancer three years earlier. He thought about different people who had made an impact on his life, but were no longer living. Suddenly he realized why he had crafted such a busy life for himself. When he stayed busy, he could suppress the thought of his own mortality. Although he logically knew that he was not invincible, he somehow managed to ignore the fact that he and his entire family would one day be gone from this earth. It would be over in the blink of an eye. Mark stood and stared at one particular tombstone, and became completely overrun with a torrent of regret. He desperately needed reconciliation with those that he hurt along his path of greed and selfishness. Mark realized he had missed the mark in life and needed forgiveness and a new direction.

Walking back to Juan, Mark said, "I noticed that every tombstone has a year of birth, year of death, full name, and words written about the person."

"Very good. How many years do you think you will live here on earth?"

"That's tough. Ideally, maybe ninety years."

"Reasonable," said Juan. "Come over here with me"

Juan led him to a back corner of the cemetery. He pointed out a grey tombstone that was completely blank. There wasn't a word or number etched into the stone. "Imagine this is your tombstone. The years etched into the stone are your own birth and death ninety years later. Now, consider the space underneath. Think about what your name would look like written in that space. Below your name, think about your epitaph. Have you ever thought about what words would be used to sum up your life on earth?"

Mark felt shell-shocked by that question. It was painful to consider what would currently be written on his tombstone. He imagined what it would look like if the engraver were honest:

Mark Davis

A husband and father of two

Neglected his family

Forgot his friends

Driven by career advancement

Lived a self-centered life

Too busy for God

Juan must have been able to read Mark's thoughts by the anguish on his face. He placed a reassuring hand on Mark's shoulder and said, "Few people take the time to honestly ask themselves that question, my friend. They live their lives and leave the summary to the engravers. But you have a choice. Right here, in this place, you can choose to change your life. **What would you like to be written on your tombstone?**"

Mark was overwhelmed by the question. He felt emotionally drained and exhausted by the fact that El Salvador had already shown his old life to be as thin as a single sheet of paper. Juan grasped Mark and gave him a strong hug. Mark could feel the love of Juan. It was genuine. It was real.

That was a weird feeling for Mark. Even as he felt his old way of looking at life crumbling around his feet, he felt surprisingly reassured. He had the thought that even a single sheet of paper can be folded into something beautiful.

⚖

The two men made it back to base camp in the early afternoon. Although he felt tired, Mark found it to be different than the exhaustion he usually felt. This was a tired brought on by the combination of physical activity and soul-searching. His usual tired was tinged with the stress of trying to constantly perform and be the best. It was a strange relief to admit that he wasn't the best.

"Take an hour or two to rest, please," said Juan. "Then we'll meet about the drilling."

"Thank you, Juan."

Juan nodded humbly.

"Just one thing," Mark said, unzipping his tent. "Even though we didn't ingest any weird plants or anything, that was still important."

Juan just laughed. "If you really listen, most hikes are," he said.

⚖

Before he let his head hit the pillow for a brief siesta, Mark opened his journal. He drew a line underneath his entry from the night before and sketched the outline of a tombstone. He left the face of it blank. Below, he wrote:

EntreBalance Principle #2:

Develop your life purpose. What would you like written on your tombstone?

He meant to ponder the question some more, but after exactly 3.5 seconds of soul-searching, he was already fast asleep.

EntreBalance Principles

1. Money is useless without time.

2. Develop your life purpose. What would you like written on your tombstone?

CHAPTER 5

It was the early afternoon, just after Mark awoke from his nap, when the meeting took place. Mark wiped something from the corner of his eyes. He wasn't sure if it was dirt or sleep residue, just that there was too much of it.

The whole crew was gathered in the dining bungalow. Uncle Thomas was entertaining Sandra and Jeremy with a story that involved him looking like he was performing the chicken dance. He flapped his imaginary wings to a chorus of Jeremy and Sandra's laughter. One of them started humming the song, so apparently the story was *about* the chicken dance. Mark gritted his teeth. He hated the chicken dance.

Tanner leaned against the far wall with a scowl that suggested he didn't appreciate the performance either. Mark began walking his way but stopped when Tanner raised a cigarette to his mouth and exhaled a cloud of smoke. Mark hated second hand smoke more than the chicken dance.

It was all starting to feel like a middle school

lunchroom. Juan was nowhere to be seen, and Mark didn't have enough of a handle on the group dynamics to feel completely comfortable yet. Up to that point, there hadn't been enough down time for Mark to feel lonely, but now he could feel the heavy tendrils wrapping around his heart.

"Shotgun or coffee?" said a voice from behind him.

Mark spun around to find Theresa smiling at him. "Huh?"

"Well, you're looking like a zombie and I figure there's only two possible solutions. Either I grab a shotgun and dispatch you in the manner I've learned from countless comic books and movies, or I grab you another cup of that horrible, terrible, *necessary* coffee."

"I choose option B," Mark said with a grin.

"Wait…does the B stand for 'BRAAAINNNS'?"

"The coffee."

"Whew. Good choice. I actually don't think I've ever even seen a firearm in real life before."

"Do I really look like a zombie?" Mark asked. He started to pat his head to see if any hairs were sticking up.

"Let's just say that you look like you've been traipsing through a cemetery all morning."

"Yeah, thanks for the warning."

"You've got to admit that it's a pretty compelling trip. Juan knows how to ask the questions that cut."

"And scar?" Mark asked.

"You'll find out," Theresa said. "I'll go grab that coffee for you."

⚖

Chapter 5

Juan entered the mess room just as Theresa brought Mark his coffee. He clapped Mark on the back as he passed. "Good afternoon, Frankenstein," he said, smiling.

Great. Frankenstein and a zombie, Mark thought. *Why are there no mirrors around?* He tried to look at his reflection in his coffee spoon. It was upside down.

"All right riffraff," Juan said from the front of the room. "I know this feels like review for many of you, but it's time to reflect on our vision."

He pulled a string and a portable screen came down at the front of the room. Juan motioned to Tanner who exited the room. The sputtering cough of a generator sounded from outside as Tanner came back to his spot leaning against the wall.

Mark suddenly felt at ease. Projector at the front of the room, warm mug of coffee in his hand, reflecting on vision: it was all very familiar to him. The corporate flavoring seemed like a handhold in the midst of the mysterious circumstances that had landed him in El Salvador. He was in his element.

Then the projector warmed up and his momentary handle dissolved like salt in a glass of water. He was used to neatly constructed power point presentations, complete with pie charts and bubble maps. Corporate vision was an ordered, safe, and rational endeavor. The projected image had none of those qualities. It looked like an explosion of words, pictures, and colors— more collage than anything else. Mark tried to take in some of the pieces. There were countless pictures of the team, some schematics, pictures of smiling villagers, two or three quotes from the Bible, a map of El Salvador—everything overlapping and running together in a cacophony of information. Mark tried to focus on just one of the pictures to make the whole image stop swirling. It was the faded picture of a young Juan leaning against the type of hand pump Mark used to see in parks when he was a kid.

"It's a bit of a mess, isn't it?" Juan asked from the front of the room. He was looking at Mark.

"What is it?" Mark asked.

"I call it my vision board. You see, I was used to casting vision from my time in the oil and gas business. Everything was ordered and had a familiar structure. I'm sure you know what I mean."

"They're safe," Mark said. "Linear."

"Exactly. *Linear*. I love that description. That was my life and vision. Linear. I was walking a straight line towards wealth, success, and recognition. But I always felt like I was missing something on the periphery. There were these shadows of people living life in a totally different way, usually without money or recognition, but they were happy."

Mark thought about his own vision. His path had been focused and singular. He had often ditched the opportunities that didn't fit within his vision of success and corporate ladder climbing. But he related to what Juan was saying. There were shadows on the periphery. Times where he felt like he was failing at life even though he was succeeding at his job. There were glimpses of other ways to live—family vacations, volunteering, helping others—that didn't quite fit into his own linear vision.

"One of the first lessons my friend Jack taught me about living in a new way was to **widen my vision**. He taught me how to include those shadows in the periphery into my vision for my life. It wasn't that wealth, success, and recognition were bad things to work toward; it's just that a full life should encompass so much more. He asked me to create a vision board, which is what you're looking at right now."

"So it's a collage?" Mark asked.

"I guess you could call it that, my friend. I tried to pull all of those shadows out of the periphery of my life and glue them down in my reality. Everything that I hoped or felt or dreamt went into the vision board. Even the tiniest inkling was documented. I didn't worry about everything fitting together or making sense. I was only concerned with getting everything nailed down. Once I finished, I began looking for threads. I was surprised to find that my home country of El Salvador and water were repeated images. This board helped me change my vision, and my life."

Mark took another look at Juan's vision board as the team began to discuss it. Instead of a swirling, confusing conglomeration of images and words, he saw the product of decades of vision planning. He began to see how Juan's vision went from a straight line to layers. Even though there was forward momentum, there was also enough room for detours and fringes.

The team discussed the vision board with passion. Mark was surprised by the fact that they spoke more about their interactions with the villagers than they did about the logistics of drilling the actual water well.

"Are you catching the vision, Mark?" Juan asked when the team's discussion was winding down.

"I think so," Mark said. "It seems like the well is just a small part of it."

"Exactly, my friend. You catch on quickly. What do

you think is the primary goal after seeing my board and hearing us talk?"

"I think it has to do with the villages."

"Perfect! In the old days, the engineering side of me would have been all about the well. How to drill it, where to drill it, how deep it should go. We still worry about all of those things, but I've added something from my periphery. Community. First and foremost we want to form lasting relationships with the villagers and with each other. Clean water is incredibly important. But love, respect, and relationships are even more essential."

"But you do drill wells, right? I don't mean to doubt, I just haven't seen any equipment or anything."

Juan let out a gruff laugh. "Of course we do. There's plenty of time for that tomorrow."

"Wait, I thought we were going to start the drilling today."

"That was the original plan, but something came up, my friend."

"More mysterious appearances from people who don't know how they got here?"

"No. We've been invited to play in a soccer game."

⚖

Mark was expecting a friendly soccer match with a couple of the local men. What he found when they arrived at the makeshift field was a crowd of at least two-hundred men, women, and children already cheering and stomping their feet.

"Is this for real?" Mark asked Tanner, who was walking next to him.

"Trust me, this is mild," Tanner said as he began to stretch.

Their rival team was already warming up on the field. It was a group of young, wiry men who had the muscles of manual laborers. Mark pinched his own corporate paunch and offered up a silent prayer for protection. He hadn't played soccer since high school.

The rules came back to him faster than the skills. Within five minutes, he was huffing and puffing after their rivals, trying to follow the ball as it danced across the field.

"Follow their hips, not the ball," Tanner joyfully shouted from somewhere on the field.

Mark couldn't understand how anyone would find a sport that was at least ninety percent running fun. Even worse was the fact that he seemed to be the team's withered limb. Even Uncle Thomas and Juan were out-performing him on the field. Everyone was smiling and laughing on both teams, which made Mark even more furious and embarrassed by his lack of skills.

Adding to his frustration was the fact that he was having a hard time processing Juan's vision board. He couldn't understand how something so messy could add depth to his life. He just wasn't ready to give up the streamlined simplicity of his own vision, yet Juan's personal story had made him uncomfortable. Mark felt like he was missing something important.

"AHHHHHH!" he yelled, barely containing a string of curses as one of the young men darted past him for the twentieth time. Someone blew a whistle and both teams retreated to separate sides of the field for a halftime break. Mark kicked at a stone in anger.

When he plopped down on the sidelines, Mark tried to control his frustration. His teammates seemed to sense what was going on and gave him a wide berth. After a minute or two, Theresa sat down beside him.

"You seem to be approaching epic levels of rage over here," she joked. "I know it's not exactly what you want to hear, but it *is* just a game, Mark."

"I don't even know what we're doing out here." Mark kept an edge to his tone, hoping Theresa would leave him alone.

"This is part of the whole vision thing. Community building."

"Don't even get me started on the vision board. How am I supposed to do something like that? I don't even *want* to make some messy vision board."

"Can I show you something?" Theresa asked. She said it with such sincerity that Mark didn't have the heart to turn her down.

Theresa grabbed her backpack and pulled out a notebook. She opened it up and passed it over to Mark. The pages featured a collage that Mark instantly knew was her vision board, but it was much more organized than Juan's. It was colorful, none of the pictures overlapped, and it was all laid out a bit like a pie chart.

"Juan's method kind of freaked me out a bit," she said. "Call me a girl if you want, but I wanted to make mine pretty."

"It looks a hundred times better," Mark confessed, "but I still don't know how it applies to me."

Chapter 5

"Let me show you two parts of my vision board,"
Theresa said. "That picture there represents a man I
met named Stephen." The picture was of a man with
a beard wearing a trench coat and fingerless gloves.
"Stephen was homeless."

"Was? So you helped him out?" Mark asked.

Theresa's mouth turned down at the edges. "No,
actually it's the opposite. I met Stephen while I was
helping with a ministry that held church services for
homeless people. I was working as a waitress, which
wasn't great money, but it gave me a lot of free time. I
could do whatever I wanted. Stephen was an alcoholic
and a drifter who didn't have anyone looking out for
him. He would show up week after week and we
would talk and tell each other jokes. When it started
to get cold out, I had the sudden vision of Stephen
sleeping in an alley with only his jacket to keep him
warm. I wanted to buy him one of those super fancy
sleeping bags." Tears were welling up in the corners of
Theresa's eyes.

"But you couldn't."

"I didn't have the money. My vision was for free
time, I wasn't used to thinking about other people."

"So what happened to Stephen?"

"I don't know. He stopped coming a few weeks
into that winter. I'm hoping that he just drifted to a
warmer climate, but sometimes I'm scared it was
much worse than that. To use Juan's words, he was in
my periphery, and I pinned him to my present. That's
where that business card comes in." Theresa pointed
to a business card for home jewelry sales that was
glued onto the pages.

"So…you bought some jewelry?" Mark asked.

"I think the terrible coffee is affecting your brain. No, I didn't buy jewelry. I started to sell it. That business card was handed to me at work. The woman said she saw something unique in me. I filed it away and forgot about it until the whole Stephen thing. When I made my vision board, I remembered it and stuck it there. I wasn't sure why, I just knew that it was important for some reason. I called the woman and started working out of home in my free time. Now I sell jewelry full time from home, and I can afford to come to El Salvador to help out."

"So the vision board helped you."

"Widening your vision isn't about creating some hodgepodge of images, despite what Juan's looks like. It's about recognizing all those good intentions you have, even the ones you've failed in, and pulling those into the forefront of your life. You have to be totally honest with yourself, and you need to listen to your heart."

The memory of his family at Disney World played out in Mark's mind once more. It was his intention to be a loving husband and father. He just wasn't always sure how that fit with his vision. In that moment, he realized that the vision he was living for was the vision of his younger self. It was the vision of the single, family-less Mark. And in that vision, his family had been pushed to the periphery.

"I think I get it," Mark said.

"I knew you would," Theresa answered. "Now it's time to widen your vision for this game of soccer."

"What do you mean?"

"You're mad because you're on the linear path of looking good and winning."

Mark knew she was right.

"Here's a little secret, Mark. They're going to kill us. They've been playing since they could walk. We're just here to laugh and have fun."

The second half of the game was a blast. Mark quit worrying about looking good and actually embraced his lack of skills. He remembered seeing the Harlem Globetrotters years ago, and he modeled his performance on the hapless other team. His falls became theatrical dives that made the crowd gasp and laugh. When one of the young men would dart past him, he would comically shake his fist at the sky before leaning over to huff and puff—to the audience's delight. Soon everyone was laughing, including both teams, and Mark was greeted with a roar of delight when he accidentally scored a goal on his own team.

After the game, Juan translated for Mark as he met many of the other players and villagers. He had never been on the receiving end of so many hugs and handshakes at one time.

As he climbed into his sleeping bag that night, his bones cracked and snapped in protest. He knew the next day's work would be even more difficult, but he felt a strange sensation of peace. He wasn't used to going to bed with such a clear mind. Usually his evenings were spent fretting over the details of an upcoming sale or account. But in the midst of the symphony of animal noises, Mark felt free and light.

He opened up his journal and wrote:

EntreBalance Principle #3:
Widen your vision.

He spent a few minutes imagining what his vision board would look like, and he was ushered into a heavy sleep by images of Veronica and his smiling children.

EntreBalance Principles

1. Money is useless without time.

2. Develop your life purpose. What would you like written on your tombstone?

3. Widen your vision.

CHAPTER 6

The truck that pulled up to base camp the next morning looked ready to fall apart. It was constructed from the parts of various makes and models of trucks, and the whole piecemeal metal tapestry was seemingly held together by rust. The truck was hauling a trailer with a large piece of equipment that Mark assumed was the hydraulic drill. Joyously, each team member clambered into the bed of the truck, sitting along its edges or on top of each other. Everyone kissed their palm and slapped the side of the truck before jumping into the bed, so Mark followed suit. A giant flake of rust stuck to the spit on his hand, inciting a chorus of laughter from the team.

"Big Betty likes you, she really likes you," Jeremy laughed. "She gave you a gift."

"Umm...aren't you worried that she'll lose some more gifts?" Mark asked.

The engine croaked to life with what sounded like a dying gasp. The team high-fived each other, and the truck groaned forward.

"Don't worry, Mark," Juan called from the driver's seat. "Big Betty's usually fine as long as the roads are stable."

The roads were not stable. In fact, Mark wasn't even sure that the word *roads* applied. If he had to create a bar graph presenting roads he had experienced in his life, that trip would have been on the far side of "unstable," approaching "instant death." He white-knuckled the edge of the truck bed with every bump, lurch, and jostle. A light breakfast of eggs and bread dove and swam in his stomach full of coffee, occasionally trying to escape up his throat and out onto the road.

Mark had always found the concept of a sovereign God who has everything in His hands to be somewhat abstract. Most of the time he felt like he was the maker of his own destiny and was content to take care of himself. He would listen to testimonies of people who "found God" with a critical half-interest, wondering why everyone was so intent on giving up their own destiny to a God they couldn't see.

Then Mark experienced the "road." All of a sudden, the idea of a God who had control over everything didn't seem so abstract. There was no one else to appeal to. The rest of the team were cheering and laughing with every death-defying leap the truck took. A chunk of metal fell off the side of Big Betty, careening off into the forest with a clang. Mark realized it had to be God knitting their metal death trap together—it was nothing short of a miracle. "I don't want to die," he prayed under his breath. "Save us, save us, save us."

"Hey Mark, you okay," Tanner asked from somewhere in the truck bed.

Mark kept his eyes closed. He started to loosen his grip on the ledge in order to give a totally deceitful thumbs-up, but then they hit either a pothole or small animal and leapt into the air once more.

If this is what 'finding God' is like, Mark thought, *then I wonder what it's like to lose Him.*

⚖️

A fter what felt like too long, the truck turned onto an open field. Since it had rained the night before, Big Betty tore up the grass of the field with her mismatched tires. A horrible metallic screeching filled the air, and Mark tensed his entire body in preparation for the inevitable explosion, but it never came. Instead, Big Betty started slowing down, and Mark realized it was the sound of her brakes.

Before the truck could clamor to a complete stop, Mark rolled over the ledge of the truck bed and onto the ground. He took two steps forward and his knees buckled. He glanced back at the truck, half expecting to see it surrounded by a cloud of angels.

"We made it," he muttered in disbelief.

Juan climbed from the driver's seat and joined Mark. "Big Betty always comes through, my friend," he said. "She's as reliable now as the first day she was donated to us."

"Was it back in the 50's?" Mark asked.

"This is where I usually say something about not judging books by their covers."

"Except books don't have the potential to blow up in your face!"

"All right, crew, let's get everything unhooked," said a voice from behind Mark.

He turned to find Sandra directing the team as they assembled their equipment. Mark raised his eyebrows in surprise. "I thought you were the leader," he said to Juan.

"Only in the areas that are my strengths."

"Do you have a problem with taking directions from a woman," Sandra asked, joining them.

"No...nothing like that. It's just that Juan's been the one who..." Mark's voice trailed off sheepishly.

"It's okay, Mark, I was as surprised as you to fall into this. Trust me."

"Sandra used to be a real estate investor," Juan said. "Then her mindset changed, and she joined forces with her Uncle Thomas."

"Wait, so he's actually an uncle? I just thought that was a nickname."

Sandra laughed. "Yep, I'm the one saddled with being an actual relative of the old coot. But it worked out."

"Are you both still in real estate?"

"No, we've switched fields."

Juan laughed, but Mark wasn't sure what was so funny.

Tanner approached and passed Sandra a clipboard. "I checked everything out and your drill is good to go," he said.

"*Your* drill?" Mark asked.

"Like I said, I'm as surprised as you. I never would have thought I would be designing hydraulic drills with my half-insane uncle."

"Now you see why she's in charge," Juan said.

⚖️

Although the entire hydraulic drill was large, the actual drill bit was smaller than Mark had anticipated. He knew they would be drilling deeper than 100 feet, so he expected a bit with a significant diameter. Instead, the drill bit was about the same diameter as his arm. The metal was scratched and scuffed with the telltale marks of something that had been used often. It was hard for Mark to imagine how the actual drilling would work.

The team had already detached the trailer. They needed to drag it six feet to the exact drilling spot, and everyone, including Mark, grabbed each end of the trailer and began pushing and pulling it to the location. Mark could feel the slimy mud underneath his boots as he tried to scrape for traction, and he almost lost his balance. Everyone used all of their strength to move the drill, and people were slipping and sliding along the way. Sandra yelled out directions and encouragement as they inched their way to the exact drilling spot.

For the next five hours, Sandra relayed directions to each of the team members as they began to drill the well. Mark was taken aback by the fact that every person worked a different role for 30-minute intervals, Sandra included. He wasn't used to working on a team where no one was vying for any type of superior position and even felt a bit guilty when he took over the fun job of supervising the drill bit from Tanner. Since everyone was focused on the common goal of digging the well instead of looking out for themselves, the drilling progressed smoothly. There were two rest periods of fifteen minutes during each rotation. Mark figured it was so guys like him didn't end up in a Salvadorian hospital.

Despite the physical toll of the work, Mark was smiling the entire time. There was something strangely satisfying about watching the drill bit kick up a cloud of orange dust and dirt. In sales, there wasn't really a clear cut way to monitor progress other than by checking the money he was making the company, so it was a relief to be doing something where the effects of his labor were immediately visible. He didn't even mind the whining drone of the drill.

There was a new feeling as he lost himself in the work; a feeling that was more like a memory. As sweat dripped down his face, he wiped it with the side of his shirt and could see the mixture of water and mud. It reminded him of when he was playing in the sandbox as a little boy, when he didn't have a care in the world. The feeling washed through him like the ache in his muscles, and this time he knew what to call it. Freedom.

"Satisfying, isn't it?" Juan asked him during one of the breaks.

"Yeah. I didn't think it would be."

"No one expects it to be. Doing work like this—it's different than what most of us are used to."

"I've always kind of avoided manual labor. Even mowing the lawn. But this is different."

"It's the end result, my friend," Juan said as he pointed to the village across the field.

Mark thought about his job back home. He was successful at making money for the company and for himself, but he didn't always feel satisfied. Sometimes he would find himself closing a sale while thinking to himself, "What's the point of all of this?" He would try to chase the thoughts out of his mind through entertainment, and the paychecks would help. The well drilling was different. There was a special kind of weight to it.

"This is about **changing your mindset**," Juan continued. "We all have tremendous capacity to succeed and help others, but first we must overcome our own limiting beliefs."

"Limiting beliefs?"

"We all have certain beliefs that are almost pre-wired into our systems. Like software preloaded onto a computer. These beliefs come from any of a hundred places in life: our upbringing, economic status, religion, family, and so on. They are our beliefs about the way the world works, and they can hold us back."

Sandra approached them and passed Mark a bottle of water. "You need to stay hydrated," she said. She must have noticed the serious look on Mark's face because she immediately asked, "Is Juan giving you the change your mindset talk?"

"I think so," Mark said. "To be honest, he kind of lost me when he started talking about computer software."

"I like to think of it in terms of well-drilling," Sandra said.

"Big surprise."

"Hear me out. You can look at the dirt as your beliefs about the world, stacked on top of each other, pressed tightly together. It's pretty easy to drill through the top layers where the soil is loose, right?"

Mark remembered the drill moving pretty fast at the start of their work. It seemed to cut into the ground as if it was slicing through a cake. "Yeah, it was pretty easy at first," he said.

"That's because the top layers are the newest and loosest. The dirt and soil hasn't had thousands of years to settle. But the deeper you drill, the slower the work is. The old soil is tight and compact, as hard as a rock. It's the same for our beliefs. It's often our oldest beliefs that limit us the most. We don't want to give them up."

"That's a pretty good analogy," Mark said. "But where does the drill come in?"

"The drill is whatever it is that's changing our beliefs. When we drill down into the old dirt, it has a choice."

"It does?"

"Sure. It can either give or break our drill bit. Luckily, it usually chooses to give. It's the same for us. We can be stubborn and refuse to change our mindset, or we can give in and learn from whatever life has thrown our way."

Mark thought about how he had ended up in El Salvador in the first place. It seemed like life was using a pretty big drill in his case.

"You sound like you've been taking guru lessons from Juan," Mark said.

"I'll take that as a compliment," Sandra said. "This is just something I had to learn the hard way."

Is there ever an easy way? Mark thought to himself.

"When I was in real estate, I ran my business the way I learned it in school," Sandra continued. "I was confident, brazen, and ran a tight ship. I wasn't afraid to let someone go if they weren't pulling their weight, and everyone knew it. My focus was on sales because I learned from my father at an early age that success is measured by wealth. We matched customers to the property that would make us the most money rather than the property they needed."

It was hard for Mark to imagine Sandra as the cutthroat manager she was describing. It was the exact opposite of the humble leadership he had witnessed during the well drilling. "So were you successful?"

"Let's just say I was wealthy. Very wealthy. I just had one problem. My office had a contract with a cleaning company who would come in every night to clean. And every Wednesday, my problem came with the cleaners. His name was Joe."

"You had a problem named Joe?"

"A big problem. Joe was one of those eternally optimistic guys who seemed to have swallowed a month's worth of sunshine. He would greet me every Wednesday before going to work with his crew, and I noticed that he always volunteered for the worst possible jobs. One time I even intentionally spilled nail polish on the carpet in my office to see what he would do. Sure enough, he was all over it. You would have thought I had left a hundred dollar bill on the floor for him. Everything about Joe bugged me to no end. I didn't know how someone could be so happy doing such miserable work."

"Maybe he was on drugs," Mark offered.

"That's exactly what I thought! I even asked one of his coworkers. When they finally stopped laughing, they gave me the truth that turned Joe into a drill for my life. The coworker told me that Joe owned the cleaning company."

"He *was* on drugs!"

"The next time Joe came in, I asked him about it and he laid out his personal strategy for success. He told me that he spent most of his time managing his company and strategically planning with his board, but he dedicated 3 hours each week to working with the crew in my offices. He told me that it kept him humble and connected to the field. He also said that it was his way of modeling a servant heart for his employees. And they loved him for it. In fact, I don't think I had ever seen a cleaning crew as happy to clean as that one. It was disconcerting."

"So did you change your mindset?" Mark asked.

"Are you kidding me? Joe and his company went against everything I stood for. No, instead I tried to widen the gulf between us. I became even more shrewd and driven in my pursuit of money. I was determined to break the drill bit of Joe in my life. I even started to leave early on Wednesdays just to avoid him. But I couldn't shake that talk we had. I decided that the only way to be rid of Joe was to test out his philosophy in a way that was sure to fail. That way I could prove that it was a ridiculous business model and be done with it."

"I decided to help one of my employees by passing him a major sale. I even encouraged him to match the client to the perfect property rather than to try to upsell them. I expected the whole experiment to fail miserably. Instead, the employee sold a property, gained three new clients through a recommendation, and wrote me a thank you note for thinking of him."

"So that's when you changed your mindset?"

"Changing your mindset isn't that simple, Mark. Limiting beliefs are our deepest beliefs. Mine had ties to my father. It was terrible. Even though I was beginning to put a servant model into practice, my heart was screaming for me to just drop the whole thing. As humans, most of us would rather stay in an old system, even if it it's not working, than to change. I was no different. But I kept at it. I fought the urge to return to my old ways every single day, and eventually I started to forget the old ways. Soon my business was twice as successful as it had ever been, and my employees were happy. When I finally gave in to that drill bit named Joe, my life radically changed. I made enough to be able to semi-retire and start working with Uncle Thomas. And here I am."

"With a changed mindset?" Mark tried again, hesitantly.

"With a changed mindset," Sandra agreed.

"Doing things differently requires persistence," Juan added. "All of us are resistant to change. But look at what can happen when we stick with it." He gestured to the hydraulic drill.

"People are healed," Sandra said.

Mark wasn't sure if she was referring to the villagers or to herself. He decided she probably meant both.

⚖

The trip back to camp on Big Betty felt shorter due to everything Mark had to think about. By the time they pulled into camp, he had only imagined one scene of rusty roadside carnage. He had spent most of the ride writing down his thoughts in his journal in a bouncy scrawl. While the rest of the team climbed out of the truck bed and into the mess hall, Mark checked over what he had written. Scribbled across the top of the page was:

> ### EntreBalance Principle #4:
> ### Change your mindset.

Underneath it was the list of limiting beliefs he was aware of. He glanced over the list. "Self worth is determined by my income," "family=sacrifice," and "fear of failure" were just a few of his thoughts. He realized his awareness of many of the limiting beliefs had come from his time in El Salvador.

"El Salvador is a drill bit," he wrote at the bottom of the page. He closed his journal and put it back in his pocket before climbing from the bed of the truck. "If you don't kill me," Mark whispered to Big Betty. "I promise I'll put some of this into practice."

He kissed his palm and slapped the side of the truck.

CLANG!

A corroded chunk of the fender fell to the ground.

Mark decided it was Betty's way of solidifying the deal.

EntreBalance Principles

1. Money is useless without time.

2. Develop your life purpose. What would you like written on your tombstone?

3. Widen your vision.

4. Change your mindset.

CHAPTER 7

The next day of drilling was different. Mark survived the trip to the site, clutching the rust-pocked edge of Big Betty's truck bed with a newfound faith, only to find his legs as responsive as blocks of wood once the actual work began. He tried to hide his discomfort from the rest of the team. They seemed to be enjoying the work, diving back in as if accustomed to the daily existence of manual labor in a third world country. Tanner even sparked up a moderately cheerful sing-along to "Working in a Coal Mine" as the drill bit continued to cough dirt and dust into the air.

Mark gritted his teeth against the pain in his legs. He was helping Uncle Thomas scoop back the dirt and debris from the drill bit with a shovel. He had picked Uncle Thomas as his work partner in the hopes that it might mean a slower day. Wrong choice. Uncle Thomas worked with the strength of someone half his age—someone much younger than Mark. *Is this guy training for a triathlon?* Mark thought, annoyed that the dirt pile was much larger on his side. He paused his shoveling to try to massage some feeling back into his knees. The pins and needles stormed through his legs with the force of a hurricane.

Juan walked up to the two men and took Mark's shovel away. Mark thought about protesting in order to keep up his tough façade, but all he could do was grimace in pain.

"You look like you need a break, my friend," Juan said.

"Is it that obvious?"

"I don't mean to alarm you, but we need to avoid the Salvadorian hospitals if at all possible."

"Thanks, that doesn't alarm me at all," Mark said as he managed to bend his stiff joints enough to sit on the ground. He was so thankful to take the weight off his legs that he didn't even mind the cloud of orange dust that was hovering near his head.

"A little stiffness is normal," Juan continued. "Most of us remember the second day of drilling as the worst."

"You really know how to encourage a guy," Mark said, and both men laughed. "Seriously, though, I didn't realize I was going to be working with a professional athlete today."

"Uncle Thomas? His age has deceived all of us at one time or another. He even beat Tanner at arm wrestling the last time we drilled a well."

"Next thing you know he'll have his own shoe endorsement."

Juan looked at Mark blankly.

"Never mind."

"Is the work affecting your brain?" Juan asked.

Mark wasn't sure whether to be touched or annoyed at the genuine concern he heard in Juan's voice. "Maybe. It's just that I've never magically appeared in another country in order to drill a well before. Do you think you could take it easy on me today?"

"I know just the job."

⚖

Mark was beginning to catch on to the rhythm of well drilling in El Salvador. Rule #1: Nothing was easy—especially if Juan was involved.

For the next four hours, Mark collected soil samples in plastic baggies. It was true, the physical side of the labor was easy. The mental aspect, however, was excruciating. Juan began by giving Mark a detailed lecture on the types of soil that were conducive to successful clean water wells. It turned out that not all soil types were ideal aquifers, and there were specific parameters Juan was tracking. He was looking for loose rock and gravel, but the stones could be no greater than 1-2 cm in diameter. Any bigger gravel could potentially break the drill bit. They were avoiding any silt or clay soils as they would both have very low yields of water.

Once Mark was trained in how to recognize the different soil types and how to measure the diameter of rocks, he went to work gathering the soil samples. He collected his samples after every ten feet of drilling, filling a plastic baggie, numbering and labeling it with the depth in feet. He also analyzed the soil type and measured any bits of gravel present in the sample.

It was slow work. Although the pain in his legs was dissipating, Mark felt like he was swimming in a pool of numbers and dirt. When Sandra finally blew a whistle to signal another break, Mark had to refrain from pumping a celebratory fist in the air.

Juan brought Mark a cup of the instant coffee, and he briefly checked through the collection of plastic baggies.

"You caught on quick, my friend," Juan said. "It's not easy work."

"A-HA!" Mark shouted. "I thought you were gonna take it easy on me today?"

"Sometimes we need to think deeply *before* we can take it easy."

"That doesn't even make sense."

"Taking it easy will come when we know for sure that this will be our well."

"But I thought you picked this spot because you already knew."

"It looks good at the surface, Mark, but you're helping us know for sure. Sometimes we have to **target specific areas** to make sure we're heading in the right direction. And the right direction doesn't always fit in with conventional wisdom."

"Why do I feel another life lesson coming on?"

Juan laughed and took a sip of coffee. "Do you like fried chicken?"

Mark almost spit out his own coffee in surprise. "Are you serious? What does that have to do with drilling wells?"

"Colonel Sanders would have been great at soil sampling, my friend."

With raised eyebrows, Mark carefully searched

Juan's face for a sign that he was being duped. "Colonel Sanders? The old guy on the KFC buckets?"

"The one and only."

"So this is where you point to the hidden camera and tell me I'm on TV, right?"

"Hear me out, my friend. Colonel Sanders was more than just the face stamped on the cardboard bucket. He was a man who knew how to think deeply about specific areas of life, and he wasn't afraid to go against conventional wisdom."

"Wasn't he incredibly successful? I thought that meant he played by the rules."

"Not necessarily. At the age of 65, he had lost the motel and restaurant that was his livelihood. A highway had been rerouted, and everything he had worked for vanished. With a family to support, conventional wisdom told him to find a stable job and leave the start-up businesses to men much younger than himself."

"Sound advice since his restaurant had failed."

"Fortunately for chicken lovers everywhere, the Colonel did not give up. Instead, he targeted that area of his life and thought deeply about his passion for fried chicken. The right direction seemed to be to continue in the restaurant business. Then he surprised everyone. Instead of following the conventional wisdom being offered, he took $105 from his first social security check, packed up his car with a pressure cooker and his secret chicken recipe, and began visiting potential franchisees."

"You're kidding."

"It's too good to be true, isn't it? The larger-than-life colonel would barge into a restaurant's kitchen and set up his pressure cooker while preaching the delicious benefits of his secret recipe. Most restaurant owners were skeptical, but the end product never ceased to amaze. The Colonel would leave with his handshake franchise deal for a nickel a chicken sold. Within ten years he was making $500,000 a year in annual revenue and was able to sell the business for $2,000,000. Pretty good for a 65 year-old honorary Colonel with nothing but a chicken recipe to his name."

Mark put his hands to his forehead to massage his temples. "As much as I love a fast food lesson from a Salvadorian, Juan, I'm having a hard time seeing your point."

Juan picked up one of the bags of soil and hefted it in his palm, testing the weight. "It's what you've been doing this whole time. We need to take a soil sample every ten feet to make sure we are heading in the right direction. If we only relied on the top sample, we could end up with a broken drill, or worse, a contaminated well. Instead, we measure gravel and watch the color of the soil, looking for any telltale signs of danger. We recalibrate our drilling based on the type of soil we find. It's tough work, sure, but essential."

"Our lives are the same way. Most of us are content to pick one or two areas of life to focus on. Mine was success and recognition. We follow conventional wisdom because it's easier than targeting and analyzing the areas of life ourselves."

There was a pause as Mark felt Juan's words sink through his skin. It was true; Mark had also picked success and work as his focus in life. And he allowed conventional wisdom to lead him far away from the parts of life that mattered most. By following the model of corporate ladder climbing and moneymaking that the world seemed to value, he had alienated himself from Veronica and his kids. Now he was out of ladder to climb, and the money didn't seem to matter as much as it once did.

"But it's not just about analysis," Juan continued. "We have to be willing to go against the grain in order to improve each area of our lives. When I first came back to El Salvador, I was met with criticism from all sides. No one could understand why I would leave a top job in order to pursue water well drilling. Even the people I wanted to help would scoff at my decision. I was uncomfortable and a little depressed, but I had already targeted the area of work in my life, and I knew I had to follow through."

"As I continued to live into my new career, I realized I was still at the surface. I had to start taking samples of my soil to make sure I was heading in the right direction. I recognized that I had grown complacent in family, finances…even my own health. I began to analyze each part of my life and set goals for myself. I found that it wasn't just my career that would be unconventional; my entire life needed to change. I was scared, but it also felt freeing. I was no longer living under the weight of the world's expectations."

"Sounds nice," Mark said.

"I've never felt better, my friend. And it's not just me. Take a look at your ex-workmate." Juan motioned to where Uncle Thomas was still shoveling dirt. "Four hours later and still going strong."

"So he's a 'target specific areas' guy, too?"

"He is an expert among experts. In many things."

Uncle Thomas looked up from his shoveling and waved at the two men.

"Wait, is he like some kind of superhero?" Mark asked. "There's no way he heard us from over there."

"There's no such thing as superheroes, Mark. There are only those who are unafraid to change."

They watched as Uncle Thomas went back to shoveling the dark earth away from the drill bit. It looked like he was whistling.

"I'm sure Uncle Thomas will share with you some of his own wisdom soon," Juan said.

"As long as I don't have to arm wrestle," Mark said.

⚖️

Juan left to check up on the rest of the group, and Mark felt relieved to have a moment to himself. He pulled his journal out of his back pocket and wrote:

> ### EntreBalance Principle #5:
> ### Target specific areas.

He closed his eyes and tried to picture the areas of life that mattered most. He imagined them as baggies full of issues, thoughts, and complacencies that he needed to analyze. There was a work baggy, health baggy, family, friends, and finances. Soon he was scribbling thoughts and ideas as fast as his pen would let him.

The work excited him. It had been a long time since Mark had felt so inspired—long enough for him to almost forget the feeling altogether. He was so involved in his journal that he failed to notice the shadow that blocked out the afternoon sun.

"Ahem."

Mark quickly slammed his journal shut and glanced up at a smiling Uncle Thomas. He was drenched in sweat but was still wearing a smile that threatened to break out in laughter at any minute. Laughter or the chicken dance.

"Care if I borrow you for a minute or two?"

Mark realized he was flexing his arm muscle. Visions of Uncle Thomas snapping his arm like a chicken bone in an epic arm wrestling match danced through his head.

"Don't worry," Uncle Thomas said. "It's nothing dangerous."

That's when Mark really started to worry.

EntreBalance Principles

1. Money is useless without time.

2. Develop your life purpose. What would you like written on your tombstone?

3. Widen your vision.

4. Change your mindset.

5. Target specific areas.

CHAPTER 8

Uncle Thomas led the way through the bustling noise of the work site. Mark glanced nervously to his left and right, trying to locate the flat surface or tree stump they would use for their arm wrestling match. He was surprised when their journey ended back at the drill.

"I promise there won't be any shoveling this time," Uncle Thomas shouted over the throbbing sputter of the hydraulic motor. "I just need your help monitoring the drill for a moment."

Mark tried not to let his face register any surprise. "That's it?"

"What, did you think we were going to arm wrestle or something?" Uncle Thomas asked with a wink.

"No...I..."

"We'll save that for tonight." The old man slapped Mark across the back with gusto. "Right now I need you to watch the drill. I have to go help Tanner put together some piping, but we can't leave the drill

81

unattended. Just watch and listen. If anything seems like it's going wrong, hit that big red button over there."

Uncle Thomas pointed at the button. To Mark, it seemed like one of the doomsday buttons presidents always had in movies.

"But how will I know if something is going wrong?" Mark asked.

"You're married right?"

"Yeah."

"How do you know when something's wrong with your wife?"

"She tells me."

Uncle Thomas let out a laugh that Mark was pretty sure could qualify as a *guffaw*. "But what about when she doesn't just tell you?" the old man asked.

Mark thought about it for a moment. "I guess her actions still kind of tell me. She acts weird."

"Exactly. Hit that red button if the drill sounds or acts weird. I'll be back in a minute."

Sounds easy enough, Mark thought. *Better than stuffing dirt in Ziploc bags. Besides, what's the worst that could happen?*

"Oh, one more thing," Uncle Thomas said, as if on cue. "If you see any flames or anything, don't worry about the button. Just run."

As Uncle Thomas turned to walk away, he began to tunelessly whistle a song. The Chicken Dance.

This is how nightmares begin, Mark thought, *with flammable machinery and horrible polka songs.*

⚖

The drill turned out to be much less flammable than Uncle Thomas's warning suggested. Mark quickly learned the pattern of the whirring vibrations of the drill bit. There was a steady rhythm as the drill lifted and pushed back into the earth, slowly grinding its way deeper with each plunge. Even though the stammer of the motor was overwhelmingly loud, the underlying rhythm was as peaceful as a nursery rhyme. Mark allowed the waves of sound to carry him deep inside himself.

Veronica's face when she was angry. That's what bounced through Mark's mind. The splotches of red on her cheeks when Mark missed dinner. The slight downward curve of the edges of her mouth when he lost patience with the kids. The shimmery wetness of her eyes when he had to cancel another date night for work. Mark was very familiar with the way anger and disappointment distorted her beauty, especially recently.

And he was the cause of it. He always knew that, but he had been able to rationalize her anger as a small sacrifice for later wealth, success, and happiness. He figured she would soon forget all his missteps along the way and instead be grateful for the material comfort he could provide.

The problem was that El Salvador was changing something inside of him. It was as if the years of self-delusion and misguided aspirations were walls that were coming apart brick-by-brick. As Mark thought about his purpose and vision for his life, he knew that his wife's anger was not some bump in the road—it was a reality that he would have to work hard to undo.

As the drill continued its monotonous thumping

into the ground, Mark pulled out his journal and decided it was time to take the drill to his own life. With his wife's angry face as inspiration, he began to sketch thoughts about how to revise his life. How could he soften that anger and once more promote the vivacious beauty she had once offered the world?

Mark began with a quarterly goal. He had never been much of a goal-setter at work, preferring to let the company set his monthly sales challenges. But this was different. This was the livelihood and happiness of his family. He knew that he would need to begin with something concrete and achievable. To let Veronica down anymore could bring disaster.

Mark's goal slowly began to emerge from the thoughts, scribbles, and sketches of his brainstorming session. 10 date nights in the quarter. 15 family dinners. Attending his children's programs when he was in town. Cutting back to one late night a week at work.

The floodgates of revelation opened, and Mark lost himself in the frenetic capturing of ideas on the page. It was as if the rhythms of the drill were increasing to match his inspired scribbling. Everything seemed to be reaching a crescendo—louder and faster.

KA-CHUNK!

Mark looked up from his page. *That was a new sound.* KAAA-CHUNKKKK! The hydraulic motor seemed to lift into the air, balancing on the drill bit. The machine shuddered and whined. It was definitely doing something weird.

KA-CHUNK! KA-CHUNK! KA-CHUNK! The drill seemed to slow, then speed up, rocking the motor back and cracking it onto the ground. Mark threw his journal behind him and ran toward the drill. The machine was like a bucking bronco. Mark gritted his teeth against the piercing squeals. He was vaguely aware of the rest of the team running towards him, but he already knew what he had to do. He leapt into the air and punched the red button on the side of the drill.

The drill let out one final exhale, a giant *whoosh*, before slowing to silence. The rest of the team surrounded Mark and the drill.

"What happened?"

"Is it okay?"

"Did it break?"

Mark searched the panicked faces for Uncle Thomas. Explanations shot through his head, but he knew there was no excuse for writing in his journal instead of watching the drill. He had shirked his one responsibility, and now the entire project could be in jeopardy.

Uncle Thomas pushed his way to Mark through the rest of the team. "What happened Mark?" he asked.

"Everything was going great, so I kind of started to jot down some notes in my journal. Then the drill started acting weird, so I hit the button."

"How weird?"

"Bull-with-a-bee-in-its-ear weird."

Juan spoke up from where he was inspecting the hole. "Maybe we hit a boulder?"

"That would make sense," Uncle Thomas grunted. He snaked the drill bit from the hole and checked it over. Then he restarted the motor and inched the drill over a couple of inches. The machine was calm—no signs of bronco bucking.

Uncle Thomas wiped his hands on his jeans and said, "Everything looks okay. We're lucky Mark shut her down when he did."

The team broke out into cheering and hugs. Mark's hand had never been subjected to so many high fives at once. Soon the team was back at work at their various posts. Only Juan and Uncle Thomas stayed behind.

"I believe you dropped something, my friend," Juan said as he handed Mark his journal. There was a new layer of dirt covering it. "Now it looks as battle-worn as you."

"Battle-worn—ha. I feel more like I'm shell-shocked."

"But you saved the day."

"More like I averted a disaster that I was partly to blame for."

"And you learned something."

"Like don't drift off into la-la land when operating heavy machinery?"

"That's a good lesson," Uncle Thomas added, "but I think Juan's thinking more about a lesson in accountability."

"Exactly, my wise friend. Mark, this is the perfect example of why **accountability is key.**"

Mark held up a stinging palm. "Wait a sec, guys. I don't think I'm ready to learn another lesson right now. I almost let our drill blow up in my own face."

Juan and Uncle Thomas laughed. "But this is the perfect time," Juan said. "You've already learned the lesson. All we need to do is put words to it."

Mark looked at Uncle Thomas. "I'm not getting out of this one, right?"

"Afraid not, son. Juan's got a point. This is a low-hanging-fruit type of lesson."

"Okay, I give in. Can we just talk someplace away from the drill? I think I've had my fill of supervision for the day."

"Sure thing, my friend."

⚖

Tanner graciously, if a bit begrudgingly, handed over his job to the three men in order to go supervise the drill. Mark, Juan, and Uncle Thomas sat on the ground and continued to fold a stack of pamphlets written in Spanish. They were covered in cartoon depictions of people drawing water from a well.

"What are these about?" Mark asked.

"They are pamphlets about how to use and fix the well," Juan answered. "They also tell people good tips on how to keep their water free from contaminations."

"The pamphlets help educate the villagers and also give them the responsibility of caring for the well. We want to hold them accountable for their new clean water," Uncle Thomas added.

"There's that accountable word again."

"My friend, you just saw a benefit to accountability. The drill was working on its own, and it would have kept pounding at that boulder until it broke if you hadn't stopped it. It needed your outside influence to save it from itself."

"As humans, we are the same way. We get stuck in our routines, just like we talked about. And even though we would want to break free, we can't without help from the outside."

Mark thought about it as he folded more pamphlets. One showed a cartoon character repairing a crack in the well casing. "So you're saying we all need accountability from someone to help us succeed?"

"That is part of it, my friend. I think there are three levels to accountability. The first is **personal accountability**."

"Where you hold yourself accountable?"

"Exactly. Many of us practice this on a daily basis through goal setting and pushing ourselves to succeed."

Mark thought of the goals he had been working on before the drill went crazy. "Yeah, I'm pretty familiar with personal accountability," he said.

"But look at what happened with the drill," Juan continued. "You were holding yourself accountable to look after the drill, but your mind drifted. You said so yourself."

"I just fell into the demented rhythm of the thing. If it wasn't going to ultimately provide water for these people, I would swear it was evil."

The three men laughed as they continued to fold and stack their pamphlets.

"Let me ask you a question," Uncle Thomas said. "Would you have drifted off if I had stuck around?"

"Probably not."

"Most of us are the same way," Juan said. "We need another person to help hold us accountable. That's **one-on-one accountability**. Usually we need someone who we feel safe and comfortable with. Someone who will encourage us to succeed and who will be there for us if we fail. This can be a spouse, good friend, or even a co-worker or peer. We want it to be someone who can give us a new perspective."

"So Uncle Thomas was my one-to-one accountability."

"I'm the one you would've had to answer to if that drill bit broke," Uncle Thomas replied. "And let's just say our arm wrestling match wouldn't have been civil."

Mark smiled nervously, and tried to forget the fact that Uncle Thomas wasn't smiling in return. "What's the third type of accountability?" he asked.

"**Group accountability**," Juan answered. "That's where we find a group of people with similar goals and we all hold each other accountable. It's where we know each other's struggles because they are our own struggles. So we also know how to encourage each other."

"Like a water well drilling team?"

"Exactly, my friend. You catch on fast."

Mark finished folding his last pamphlet and set it on top of the stack. "I see how this applies to what we're doing here in El Salvador, but what about normal life?"

"I can answer that," said Uncle Thomas. "I've taken accountability very seriously with many of my businesses. In fact, I think accountability has been one of the sole reasons I've succeeded. I didn't always take it seriously. Most of my early years in real estate were spent floundering from one client to the next. Then I remembered basketball."

"Basketball?"

"Basketball. I know it doesn't look like it now, but when I was in high school, I was an all-state champ."

Are you kidding me? Mark thought. *Based on the ripped-old-guy thing you have going for you right now, I'm surprised you didn't just take on the whole state by yourself.*

"I remembered how I met my goal of being a great basketball player," Uncle Thomas continued. "It started with setting personal speed, shot, and weight training goals. That was the easy part. But then I started working out with some guys from the team who also had some serious goals. We ended up pushing each other to new heights through healthy competition and encouragement. We also had a great coach. He was the one who could see all of our faults better than we could, and he pushed us to improve very specific parts of our game. So I had it all—personal, group, and one-to-one accountability."

"And it sounds like it worked out for you in high school," Mark said.

"Not just high school. I ended up using the same accountability structure with my business. I set personal goals and tracked my daily progress. I met with other local businessmen monthly to discuss how things were going. I even hired an outside business coach to help me see where I could improve. Next thing I knew, my businesses were taking off."

"What about El Salvador?"

"This is where my goals and trajectory brought me. I couldn't be happier. It figures that I had to find some old coot who's even crazier than me." Uncle Thomas wrapped an arm around Juan's shoulders. "But I have to say I still drive the better truck."

"Shh…" Juan said. "Big Betty might hear you."

Mark packed up the pamphlets into a nearby

suitcase. "I don't think you need to worry, Juan," he said. "Big Betty's ears fell off years ago."

⚖

Back at the camp, Juan gave everyone the evening off to rest and recuperate. They had finally struck clean water, and the next day would be the unveiling of the well. Mark seized the opportunity to continue planning out his future goals. On the side of the paper, he wrote:

> ### EntreBalance Principle #6:
> **Apply personal, one-on-one, and group accountability.**

Underneath each heading he listed names of people he could trust to help him reshape his life with his family.

The camp filled with laughter as somebody started an impromptu soccer game. Mark marveled at the idea of anyone running after such a hard day's work. The shouts and giggles reminded him of home, and his heart felt heavy in his chest.

Mark looked at his goals and aspirations—they were the footprints of a changed man. He prayed that it wasn't too late. He had to get home to Veronica and the kids because he knew he had been away for far too long.

EntreBalance Principles

1. Money is useless without time.

2. Develop your life purpose. What would you like written on your tombstone?

3. Widen your vision.

4. Change your mindset.

5. Target specific areas.

6. Apply personal, one-on-one, and group accountability.

CHAPTER 9

Mark awoke the next morning to thoughts of his family hovering in the air above him. Veronica and his kids seemed close enough to touch, smiling proudly at him the way they used to, but then they were gone. Mark was alone in his pitch-black tent; the only sound a gentle flapping of a loose canvas corner in the wind.

He stumbled around the tents of his sleeping teammates to the little bunker. A faint yellow light leaked from the cracked doorframe, and Mark could barely make out Juan seated at a bench, sipping some coffee.

"Good morning, friend," Juan said as Mark lurched into the room. "Coffee?"

Mark accepted a fresh mug. "Look, Juan," he said, "I don't belong here. I need to get back to my family."

"I know you miss your family, Mark, and I'm sure they miss you, too. But I disagree."

Uh oh, Mark thought, *this is where the horror movie twist comes in—when they lock me in a cage or feed me to the villagers.* "You can't force me to stay!"

"That's not what I mean. You said you don't belong here, but *here* you are. You helped us dig a well."

"But now we're done. We found the clean water."

"That's a good start, my friend, but there's more to be done. We would like you to stay."

"You don't need me, though. You've got plenty of hands."

"It's not about need at this point, Mark. It's about seeing this through to the end."

Mark knew Juan had a point. He had made it this far and learned some life-altering lessons along the way. But he couldn't shake the thoughts of his family that clouded his mind. What if they were out looking for him? What if they never received his e-mail?

Juan tipped his coffee back and finished it with a giant gulp. "I know that you're anxious to get home, and we won't stop you. My computer is plugged in and connected to the satellite over there," Juan motioned to the corner. "But if you can stay, we still need your help." The old man stood, stretched, and walked out the door, leaving Mark alone with the computer and his thoughts.

Oh, great, Mark thought, *the oldest trick in the book.* He was familiar with Juan's technique—state a desired outcome, express possible disappointment, leave person alone with their thoughts—Mark had used it himself with a couple of his employees. *It's not going to work on me,* he decided. He walked over to the computer and turned it on. As the screen came to life, Mark was struck by the computer's background image. It was a picture of the team—sans Mark—

along with at least fifty smiling villagers, everyone standing around the shiny metal pump of a new well. Mark couldn't help but think of the transformative power of that one hole in the ground. Children could be saved from death. Men and women would have clean water to drink, cook with, and wash their everyday wounds.

Mark wasn't sure whether the picture was part of Juan's plan. If so, he was an even craftier old Salvadorian than Mark had originally thought. He sighed, shut off the computer, and jogged out the door to catch up with Juan.

The old man was throwing shovels and heavy burlap bags into the back of Big Betty. He turned and smiled when he heard Mark approaching.

"At what time are you leaving us, my friend?" Juan asked.

"Okay, okay. You can have my expertise for one more day," Mark said. "But that's it! I'm leaving tomorrow and no sentimental picture is gonna keep me here."

"Perfect. One day is all we need. Now, you can help me load up Big Betty with this cement mix."

"Cement mix?"

"There's no better way to wake up in the morning than to mix a little cement. Oh, and you'll need this." Juan handed Mark something that looked like a gas mask. "The cement dust can be dangerous to breathe."

For a second, Mark debated running back to the computer and booking his tickets. Then Juan thrust a huge bag of cement mix into his arms. He climbed into the truck bed with an odd combination of excitement and acceptance. By day four, it was a familiar feeling—a feeling he would always associate with El Salvador.

⚖

Just before Juan and Mark took off for the drill site, Tanner climbed into the truck with them. He slammed the passenger door with a grunt. "Couldn't sleep," he said. He immediately rolled down his window and lit a cigarette.

"Isn't it kind of early for that," Mark asked.

"I'll be nicer."

Mark looked to Juan for help, but the old man just shrugged his shoulders. Tanner exhaled smoke out his open window.

"Look," Tanner said, "let's cut a deal. You don't mention my bad habit, and I won't mention how you almost let the drill explode yesterday."

"Fair enough."

Mark rode the rest of the way to the well in silence, enjoying the untainted morning air that drifted through Juan's window. *I hope he gets nicer,* he thought as Tanner savored his morning smoke.

⚖

The work site was littered with remnants of the job: stray tools, piping, casing, and even a bag or two of soil samples. Mark knew that the site would be cleaned up when the rest of the team arrived, but the eeriness was a bit unsettling. It was like a non-profit ghost town.

Tanner must have felt the same way because he

began to whistle a low, eerie tune. He looked at Mark with raised eyebrows, and they broke out laughing.

"You're right," Mark said, "you *are* nicer."

"And to think this could have all been one giant crater," Tanner laughed. "Good thing you snapped out of it when you did."

"Gentlemen," Juan interrupted. He pointed to the bags of mixed cement and a hose he had attached to the water flowing from the well. "It's time to flex our muscles."

"Couldn't we have brought in a mixer?" Mark asked.

"We don't need that much cement," Tanner said as he pulled his respirator over his face, the material muffling his voice. "Besides, this is your chance to outwork my vice-ridden lungs."

"You're on."

For the next hour, the three men mixed the cement on the ground. Juan was in charge of measuring out the mixture and water, while Tanner and Mark stirred and pushed the resulting slop with their shovels. A steady cloud of dust blurred their vision, and Mark was glad for the respirator. The cloud mixed with the debris of the worksite made him feel like he was participating in an archeological dig.

After most of the mixture had been added, Juan left with Big Betty to pick up the rest of the team. Mark and Tanner kept at the cement with their shovels. Mark was impressed with Tanner's perseverance. He could hear the man's heavy breathing through his respirator, but Tanner did not complain or stop to rest once.

The rest of the team arrived and began carting

the cement over to the hole where they were setting up the pump for the well. Uncle Thomas and Jeremy took over their shovels, and Mark collapsed onto the ground, thankful for the break. He looked over to his right and saw Tanner marking something in a journal just like his own.

"Deep thoughts?" Mark asked.

"Checklist. I'm crossing out one of the team's daily goals—cement mixing."

"You have daily goals?"

"Of course! I'm all for quarterly goals and big picture planning, but the monthly, weekly, and daily are where the nitty-gritty happens."

"Sounds a little OCD to me."

Juan walked up to the two men and passed them each a bottle of water. "It's not well water yet, but we'll have some soon," he said.

"Good old delayed gratification," Mark said.

Juan and Tanner looked at each other and back at Mark with slight frowns.

"What? Do I smell?" Mark sniffed his armpits.

"No, it's not that, my friend," Juan said. "It's just that you said something no good."

"Wait, did I cuss by accident? I do that sometimes?"

"Worse than cussing," said Tanner. "You said the d-g word."

"You mean the g-d word?" Mark asked, confused.

"No, the d-g word," Juan answered. "Delayed gratification."

"You guys are kidding me, right? Since when is that a bad word?"

"It's not so much that it's a bad word as it's not an *ideal* word," Juan said. "I think we can all agree that instant gratification is a major problem. The massive debt problems in your country alone can serve as a testimony to that fact."

Mark thought about his friends, family, and co-workers who were in debt. Many of them would purchase items as soon as they felt desire—which was usually after watching a television commercial or seeing someone else using one. He remembered the "Black Friday" pandemonium he had seen on the news. It was hard to argue against the fact that the US was obsessed with instant gratification. Still, that had never been Mark. He had always been one to save and plan for the future.

"Sure, the US has a problem with instant gratification," he said. "But that doesn't explain how delayed gratification is—in your words—'not ideal.'"

"Delayed gratification is a knee-jerk reaction to instant gratification," Juan continued. "They're opposite sides of the scale. Delayed gratification can be exceptionally useful in certain situations, like getting out of debt, but many of us take it to an extreme. Mark, allow me to use your story as an example. You told me that you wanted to become the President of your beverage company, and that's why you sacrificed for so many years and spent all your time away from your wife and children. You were obsessed with delayed gratification. You sacrificed too much to achieve your long-term dream. In fact, you later discovered that your long-term dream would never become a reality."

Juan's words stung, but Mark knew it was only because they were true. He *had* sacrificed too much for a dream that amounted to nothing. "So what's the alternative, then? What's at the middle of the scale?" he asked.

"Balanced gratification."

"Makes sense."

"It works like the cement we've been mixing. If we just let the cement sit for a few hours before taking it over to the well, it would set. Then it would be impossible to move it or use it for our purposes. Instead, we keep stirring it to make sure it doesn't set. We move it bit by bit over to the well pump. Balanced gratification allows for a type of gradual release. Instead of forsaking friends and family for the end goal of promotion, we look at our lives, determine what's important, and then create boundaries around those things. We can still make sacrifices, but not to the extremes that delayed gratification often demands. And there are little successes—rewards—along the way to encourage us."

"So delayed gratification is like the cement that sets?"

"And balanced gratification is the constantly moving cement. Exactly."

"That's where my daily goals come into play," Tanner added. "My monthly, weekly, and daily goals are where I can create the boundaries for delayed gratification. I schedule meetings and time with important clients, but I also schedule 'appointments' with family. And daily goals can help give a person that 'instant gratification' type of pleasure—without the risk. When I work with my clients, I often encourage them to create achievable daily goals in the beginning so that they have something to encourage and inspire them to stick with the program."

"Wait, you have clients?" Mark couldn't hide his surprise.

"Tanner has his own financial literacy program," Juan said. "He's even been running it with some of the villagers around El Salvador."

"I'm a little curious as to what you thought I did," Tanner said.

"I don't know...fix motorcycles, long-haul trucking...that sort of thing."

Tanner laughed. "Is it the cigarettes?"

"I guess they add to the image. I wouldn't normally expect to be taking lessons in balanced gratification from a cigarette smoker."

"Hey, I'm a work in progress. Quitting is one of my goals for the year. I've already cut down a ton. You're right, though. Cigarettes wouldn't be a good picture of balanced gratification in my life right now."

"So what is?"

"El Salvador. I wouldn't be here if it wasn't for what Juan taught me about balanced gratification. I used to be like you—a total delayed gratification nut. I had a 10-year plan of success and wealth that was all tied to my financial literacy program. I worked myself to the bone and started seeing great results. My primary clientele were college graduates and people in extreme amounts of debt, so my delayed gratification focus really worked with them. But then I started getting e-mails from this guy named Juan in El Salvador."

"I had heard of the success of his program from Uncle Thomas," Juan added. "I knew he could help many of my people learn how to wisely handle their money."

"But I was too busy to come," Tanner continued.

"I couldn't see how El Salvador fit into my long term game plan. So I just kept putting it off and making excuses. Finally, Juan just showed up—with an arsenal of pictures, information, and convicting advice."

"I can relate," Mark said.

"Juan showed me the concept of balanced gratification. He helped me see all the areas of life I was completely missing due to my obsession with delayed gratification. He helped me see that the journey was more important than the final destination. And here I am."

Mark grabbed his journal out of his back pocket and quickly wrote:

EntreBalance Principle #7:
Practice balanced gratification.

A shrill whistle cut through the men's conversation. Mark glanced up to see almost a hundred villagers gathered around the well. He had been so engrossed in their conversation that he had failed to notice the gathering crowd.

"Looks like it's my time," Juan said, excusing himself with a handshake.

Mark and Tanner joined the team at the front of the crowd as Juan was given a handheld microphone. A portable generator powered the two small speakers that began projecting his gravelly voice. As Juan gathered the crowd's attention, all of the adults took their seats on some folding chairs. The children and young adults sat in the grass or stood near their parents. As Juan addressed the crowd in Spanish, everyone suddenly looked toward Mark's group and began to cheer. Juan explained in English that they were cheering for all of the hard work that went into the construction of the well. Juan then returned to speaking to the crowd in Spanish, and Mark could only recognize the occasional word. He slowly came to understand that Juan was telling a story from the Bible. In the story, Jesus met a woman at the well and offered the confused woman "living water."

Mark shifted his attention to the shiny metal pump. The handle gleamed in the sun, and he could imagine the hundreds of hands that would grasp it with hope and thankfulness for many years to come. He thought about the team and everything he had learned from them. Everyone was so different— from the boisterous Uncle Thomas to the youthfully sarcastic Theresa—but they each brought something essential to the team. And they all worked together beautifully.

Mark realized he had experienced a new form of community that was fed by a mindset completely different than his own. And it wasn't just Juan's beliefs—it seemed like the ideas flowed from some place deeper and more primary. Mark knew he wanted to live life the way his new friends did, and he knew the steps he had to take.

A firm grip on his forearm broke him from his revelry. Juan pulled him to the front of the group as the villagers and team cheered on.

"Mark, you have truly been a godsend to our team. Without you, this well would not be here. Will you do us the honor?" Juan asked.

Mark felt a lump forming in the back of his throat, and he wiped at his eyes with his sleeve. "Of course."

Juan pumped the handle for about a minute until the clearest water Mark had ever seen poured from the spout of the pump. The crowd erupted. Someone passed Mark a glass and he stuck it in the stream, allowing the cool water to flow over his hand.

He turned to the crowd, looking each of his new friends and teammates in the eye. "To fresh, new life," he said.

He closed his eyes, tipped back his head, and let the water pour down his throat.

EntreBalance Principles

1. Money is useless without time.

2. Develop your life purpose. What would you like written on your tombstone?

3. Widen your vision.

4. Change your mindset.

5. Target specific areas.

6. Apply personal, one-on-one, and group accountability.

7. Practice balanced gratification.

CHAPTER 10

M ark's throat constricted into a series of gagging coughs. Disoriented, he opened his eyes to find himself lying on the ground. *How did this happen?* he thought, but his wonderment gave way to confusion and panic when he realized he was in some type of building. There were lights high above him, giving off a faint yellow glow that blurred his vision. His body convulsed into another series of coughs, and he had to turn on his side as some of the water forced its way out of his mouth.

"Sorry Juan," he managed to say between coughs, "it's not the water..."

"Oh my God, Mark," replied a voice that was distinctively *not* Juan, "are you okay? Honey, I can't believe you drank it!"

"Who...where...where's Juan?" Mark asked as he tried to sit up.

The room started slowly coming into focus. There were long wooden benches and some type of table surrounding him. He could feel hands on his shoulders and heard the hum of concerned whispers. The benches looked like the pews in his church. There was someone kneeling in front of him, and he tried to concentrate on their face, ignoring all the other confusing details. A gasp rippled through him as he realized only one brow could furrow like the one in front of him.

It was Veronica!

"Honey, take it easy. You drank some bad water and passed out. Who's Juan?"

Mark tried to compose his thoughts, but there were too many questions. "I was in El Salvador and we drilled the well and there was clean water, finally."

Veronica reached forward and pulled Mark into an embrace. "It was just a dream, Mark. You've been right here. You didn't go anywhere."

Mark felt like pulling away in desperation. Where were Juan and the team? What about the well? He reached for his journal, frantic for proof of everything that had happened, but his back pocket was empty. His whole body tensed and he felt like his world was cracking apart. Then Veronica began stroking her fingers through his hair.

"Shhh," she said, "you're okay. It's okay."

Mark felt the little hands of his son and daughter as they leaned forward to embrace him as well. The tension leaked out of his muscles, and he relaxed into his family. Proof didn't matter. Maybe it *was* all just some incredibly vivid dream brought on by bad water and missionary talk. Answers didn't matter.

He was home.

⚖

Chapter 10

M ark settled into the chair in Mr. Brenner's waiting room with an odd sense of detachment and déjà vu. After all, it had only been 24 hours since he last sat in the chair, waiting for the promotion that would never arrive. But to Mark, it felt like at least a week.

Even if his water-well adventure in El Salvador was just a dream, Mark had to admit that it changed him. He was not the same man who had sat in the chair the day before. He felt like he had a new equilibrium— one that was centered on community, family, and charity rather than greed and self-promotion. Still, there was work to be done.

Mark paused to take in the waiting room once more. There was a new lightness to everything. He didn't feel jealous or nervous or even very confident. He just felt comfortable. There was the bookcase with all of its motivational titles. Mark scanned their spines, looking for *Backpacking Through El Salvador*, but it was no longer on the shelf. Mark wasn't surprised.

Kim, the president's administrative assistant, was busy typing on her computer. She glanced up and smiled at him. "You seem in better spirits today, Mr. Davis," she said cheerily. "But you're not sporting your new watch!"

"Yeah, I decided it was more of a special occasion accessory," Mark replied. He figured it would be too confusing to go into how he had taken the watch from his wrist and donated it to the missionary at his church the night before.

"Well, Mr. Brenner is ready to see you. You may go in." Kim smiled once more and returned to her work.

Like the waiting room, the executive office was no longer as majestic or impressive as the day before.

Instead, Mark saw it for what it was: a reward for the sacrifice, hard work, and drive of one man. And it was no longer the type of reward he was looking for.

"Good afternoon, Mark, please take a seat."

"Thank you for agreeing to meet with me, Mr. Brenner. I'm sorry I left so abruptly yesterday."

"It's okay. I know it felt like we blindsided you. But before you begin, I just want to let you know that the conversation we had yesterday was one of the most difficult in my entire working career. You're a dedicated salesman, and I hated to disappoint you. But nothing has changed. Mr. Johnston's wishes are to have his relatives take over the business. I don't agree with his decision, but I respect it. I know you're a fighter and a tenacious salesman, but there's nothing you can say today that will change my mind."

"I'm not here to change your mind, Mr. Brenner."

"And please don't say anything that will jeopardize your future here. If you're considering leaving the company, please take some more time to think about it. If you simply walked out of my office right now, I would not hold it against you. I don't want you making any rash decisions."

"I don't want to leave the company."

The president looked puzzled. "Then why did you call this meeting?"

Mark took a deep breath and thought of the poverty he had experienced in his dream of El Salvador. "First, I would like to thank you for the privilege of working at this company. I'm extremely grateful that you and this company have given me the opportunity to provide for my family. I want you to know that I never want to take this job for granted."

The president's jaw dropped, and he remained speechless for several seconds. It seemed to Mark that the President was trying to figure out if he was being sarcastic or genuine. Mark smiled humbly and waited for the President to answer.

Finally, Mr. Brenner spoke. "You don't have to thank me, Mark. Your contributions to this company have been countless."

"Secondly, Mark continued, "I would like to discuss my future in the company. I noticed that there is a Training and Development Coach position that needs to be filled."

"That's true. We believe that investing in a coach could strengthen our business. Do you have someone in mind?"

"I would like to apply for the position."

President Brenner raised his eyebrows and leaned forward in his chair. "That's a totally different position than the one you have now. It's a step down."

"It would give me the opportunity to help develop people within the company. Since I have experience in many of the company's divisions, I believe I could be the most qualified to excel in that role. I would also be more than willing to help train someone to take over my current position. It sounds like Mr. Johnston is looking to have his relatives eventually fill the Vice President role, so my current position would be a good stepping-stone for them on their way to the top. I could help make that transition possible."

"It makes sense. But that position would be a significant decrease in salary."

"I understand," Mark said. "However, I would be coaching the majority of the employees Monday through Friday during normal hours. It would give me more time to spend with my family, which is my top priority, more than the money."

Before the meeting, Mark had calculated how much money he would earn in the new position. He figured out it would be significantly less per year than his current position, but if he broke that down into an hourly rate, he would actually be getting a raise. He would literally be working half the hours compared to his current position. He knew he could invest time with his family immediately. Mark thought back to Juan's advice in El Salvador: *Money, without time, is worthless.* Mark was done missing his children's sporting events, recitals, and birthday parties. There would be no more canceled date nights with Veronica.

Mr. Brenner smiled and said, "Mark, it sounds like you've given this a lot of thought. I'll discuss it with the Vice Presidents. I believe you could make an excellent Training and Development Coach. It seems like at this stage in your life and career, it would be a terrific fit for you within our company. I'm glad you scheduled this meeting."

Mark left the executive office feeling excited and alive. He no longer felt the incredible weight of trying to climb the corporate ladder. Instead of hitting a ceiling, he had widened his vision and started climbing a new ladder.

As he climbed into his car and left the office, he found himself wishing he could talk to someone from the team. *You're being crazy,* he told himself. *You made them all up.* Nevertheless, the successful first step was bittersweet. He could almost hear

Juan's deep, scratchy voice saying, "Well done, my friend."

"Well, Juan," Mark said, not caring if he looked crazy talking to thin air, "now comes the hard part. I have to tell Veronica."

⚖️

M ark nervously watched Veronica's face as the faint yellow candlelight flickered across it. They were seated at a secluded table in their favorite restaurant, *Dolce Vita*. It was the same hole-in-the-wall Italian restaurant where Mark had asked her to marry him. Although the romantic ambiance was encouraging, Mark was still about to have a minor heart attack because of the bad news he had to share.

He took a deep breath and tried to calm his heart. His hands were trembling as he poured Veronica a glass of wine and drank in how beautiful she looked in her evening dress. She caught him checking her out and smiled. He had not seen her smile in such a natural, beautiful way in many years. It was as if she were physically changing in front of him. Mark knew that she had always appreciated his confidence, but he was beginning to realize that his confidence had been replaced by egotistical cockiness a long time ago. He was trying to recapture the humility he had learned in his Salvadorian dream, and Veronica was responding like a teenage girl in love. She reached across the table and traced her fingers across his palm. Mark was surprised all over again by just how much his life was changing.

"I didn't get the promotion." The words dropped

from Mark's mouth, and he imagined them falling on Veronica's ears with a thud.

She stopped tracing his palm. "What?"

"They told me I won't ever be a VP. Johnston's saving the positions for his relatives."

"Are you kidding me? After all your work… the nights…the traveling?!" Veronica's voice raised in pitch, and Mark caught himself involuntarily flinching.

"I know, I was mad, too. But something came up. It's that weird dream I had, the one from the water."

"Don't start, Mark."

"Hear me out. It's like I was shown a new way of living life. I could see all of my mistakes—how much I had let you down. So I took a new job. It just went through today. I took a pay decrease, but there's no more traveling. It's 9 to 5. I don't want to be the absent moneymaker anymore. I want to go on trips. I want to go to school events. I'm not giving Mr. Johnston all of my hard work anymore. I want to give it to you."

Veronica was silent. Mark swallowed nervously as she just looked at him. He couldn't figure out her look—her expression seemed blank. Then a grin spilt across her face. The grin broke into a smile. Soon she was beaming as tears streamed down her cheeks.

"Why are you—"

"Shhh," Veronica interrupted. "Just be quiet. I've been waiting so long for you to say those words. I want to listen to them echo."

They sat facing each other in the glow of the candlelight—Mark silent and Veronica beaming and crying. The restaurant seemed to melt into the shadows until it was just the two of them—a husband and wife—crying and laughing with rekindled love.

⚖

After Mark widened his vision and freed up his time, he began working on his goals. He found a local group of entrepreneurs who were already hosting monthly accountability meetings. He found a coach who helped him set goals for all areas of life, including his business, family, and personal growth.

As the months passed and Mark lived out his new vision and direction, he realized his story could help other people as well. He began constructing a plan for a series of talks, all based around the concepts he learned in his dream. Soon he was booking motivational talks on his weekends. He found that many people could relate to the truths he had learned in his dream.

It wasn't until his second month of completely booked weekends that Mark realized his talks could turn into a viable business. He loved being able to take his family with him to conferences all over the country, and there seemed to be a large market and hunger for the lessons he was sharing. Mark was able to start paying off his debts with the proceeds from the talks, which allowed him to cut back on his hours at his day job. He loved the challenges of starting his own business and found that it added excitement and value to his working life.

But he couldn't ever mention the dream. He had tried to bring it up with Veronica a couple of times, but she would immediately grow uncomfortable. He learned that it was better to talk about *what* he had learned rather than *how* he learned it. The hardest part was accepting praise for ideas that still didn't seem to belong to him. Many nights, after finishing another talk, Mark would catch himself wishing he could call Juan up and thank him for everything.

One Saturday night, Mark was finishing up a speech in Houston. He was at his favorite part of the speech—when he compared his previous life to drinking dirty water. He likened his selfish, greed-centered life to skimming contaminated water from the surface of life. But then he learned about the clean water that was far below the surface. It was hard work to reach, but when he did, he found a truly refreshing life.

It was Mark's way of paying tribute to where his ideas came from, dream or not. As he finished sharing about his new, deeply refreshing approach to life, he noticed a familiar face as he scanned the crowd. It took a moment for his brain to register the recognition, and he almost fell backwards onto the stage. He scanned the crowd once more, and there he was—third row from the front, with a huge smile playing across his wrinkled face. Juan.

Mark's mind reeled. He rubbed his eyes, but Juan was still there, grinning and waving. Mark tried to block the impending breakdown of reality long enough to finish his talk. As soon as he was done, he leapt from the stage and made his way to Juan. He reached him while there was still some lingering applause.

"Hello, my friend," Juan said. It was the exact voice Mark remembered from his dream.

"But…how…what…" Mark stammered.

"You left so quickly, we didn't have a chance to say goodbye," Juan said.

"But you're just a dream."

Juan laughed. "I may have been called dreamy back in my day, but never a dream."

"The well?"

"It's doing great, my friend! I am now organizing the next project. It's part of why I wanted to hunt you down. That and you forgot this."

Juan pressed something into Mark's hands. It was his journal.

"This is all too weird," Mark said.

"I took the liberty of flipping through it, I hope you don't mind. There are too many good things for that journal to go to waste, Mark. Although it sounds like you've already put much of what you learned into practice."

Mark briefly flipped through the journal as his memories of El Salvador washed over him. When he looked back at Juan, he had to brush the tears from the corners of his eyes.

"Will you think about joining us again, my friend?" Juan asked. "You could bring your family."

Before Mark could answer, a crowd of people surrounded him, clapping him on the back and wanting to shake his hand. The well-wishers pushed between him and Juan in a flurry of movement, and by the time Mark broke through their congratulations, Juan was nowhere to be seen.

Soon the crowd of attendees dissipated, leaving Mark alone in the room with the cleaning crew. He sat in one of the chairs and thumbed through his journal. The sound of the vacuum cleaners was a soothing soundtrack to his journey back through all that he had learned.

EntreBalance Principles:

1. **Money is useless without time.**

2. **Develop your life purpose. What would you like written on your tombstone?**

3. **Widen your vision.**

4. **Change your mindset.**

5. **Target specific areas.**

6. **Apply personal, one-on-one, and group accountability.**

7. **Practice balanced gratification.**

The last pages of the journal had been filled out by another hand. Mark knew the scratchy cursive letters were Juan's. A picture of the team standing in front of the well had been pasted in; Mark figured one of the villagers had taken it on the last day. He squinted his eyes and looked closely. Sure enough, he recognized himself squatting in the middle of the group, looking tired and scrappy in his hand-me-down work clothes. *Wait until Veronica sees this!* Mark thought.

Underneath the picture, Juan had written:

You were truly a godsend, my friend. We do not know how you came to be a part of our team, only that you were essential for the success of the well. I pray that you found your time in El Salvador to be eye opening and refreshing. We miss you dearly and hope you can find time to join us on the next project. Maybe you can plan for this trip instead of just appearing. We would love for your family to be a part of the work as well.

If you remember the words and ideas of a crazy, old Salvadorian man like me, that is proof of miracles in this world. May your life be full of deep, refreshing satisfaction.

I read this quote many years ago, and I want to pass it on to you. Carry it close, my friend.

—Juan

The cleaning crew had finished their work, and Mark was alone in the giant room. He was glad there was no one around to see the tears soaking his cheeks. He brushed at his eyes once more and turned to the last page of the journal. The quote was scrawled across the page in Juan's wide, looping script.

*"Something of God flows into us from the blue of the sky, the taste of honey, **the delicious embrace of water whether cold or hot,** and even from sleep itself."*

—C.S. Lewis

Thanks so much for reading my book! I hope that you enjoyed it and are applying the EntreBalance Principles to your life.

As a bonus, I have also included a number of free tools on my website. The resources will give you more tangible ideas and specific direction on how to achieve EntreBalance. Just visit www.JaredPolak.com and immediately begin implementing the principles to balance your life and pursue an entrepreneurial mindset.

Best Regards,
Jared Polak.

www.ingramcontent.com/pod-product-compliance
Lightning Source LLC
Chambersburg PA
CBHW030842090426
42737CB00009B/1073